FULL MOON

BY NORMAN KRASNA

DRAMATISTS
PLAY SERVICE
INC.

CAST

(In Order of Appearance)

CATHY TEMPLE

DAVID DILLON

CRYSTAL LEROY

COLONEL TEMPLE

SCENES

The action takes place in a converted apartment in the Village.

The time is the present.

ACT ONE

Scene 1: Five P.M. on a day in May.
Scene 2: Three weeks later. Eleven A.M.
Scene 3: The following morning. Nine A.M.

ACT TWO

Scene 1: Two days later. Midnight.
Scene 2: The following day. One P.M.
Scene 3: The same night. Midnight.

FULL MOON

ACT ONE

SCENE 1

The Curtain Rises on the living room of a single apartment in the Village. The building was a large, private home fifty years ago and has been altered to accommodate multiple tenants. The ceiling is high, the walls are panelled. The second floor windows, Right, are separated by a fireplace and a good mantel, Center, Rear, is an open bar, with practical sink, converted from a pantry, through which one passes to the kitchen. Left, Rear, is the hall into the bedroom and bathroom. Left, is the apartment entrance, directly off the outside stairs. There is a speaker plaque in the wall beside the door, to communicate with arriving guests. Framed sketches of stage sets on the walls, some water colors and oils by Village artists. A typewriter and writing material are on a desk near the window, on which sits a large pile of new books. Also a telephone with a long cord which plugs into the wall, the type that can be unplugged.

A table, Center, functions as the dining area, with light chairs pushed into place when necessary. An easy chair and a forward couch are colorfully covered. The couch can be made into a bed. A carpenter-made shelf of books and some group photographs reflect loving hands.

At the moment the Set is lighted only from what can filter in through the windows at five o'clock on a day in May.

We hear the key in the door and Cathy Temple enters, flicking the light switch on, and holding the door open for David Dillon.

First, Cathy. She's twenty-three, bright, alert, has a strong yet appealing face, a trim figure, and exudes a scrubbed cleanliness usually seen on soap advertisements. David is two years older, a most personable young man and if there was a man next to the girl on the soap advertisement, the advertising agency would have picked him. The reason they are exactly this attractive is because they are actors, which we will soon discover. They carry scripts.

CATHY. (*Letting David enter.*) And here we are. Chez moi. (*David enters, Cathy closes the door behind him.*)
DAVID. (*Looking about, most impressed.*) Ho, ho! Some chez!
CATHY. (*Pleased.*) Thank you.
DAVID. A fireplace and panelling! Does it work?
CATHY. Well, the panelling works, the fireplace smokes a little.
DAVID. How the devil did you find it? And how can you afford it?
CATHY. I inherited it from a girl I knew at Actors Lab. She got a movie contract and had to leave for the Coast in twenty-four hours. And I can't afford it.
DAVID. You lucky stiff!
CATHY. You bet. This was the dining room of the family that lived here sixty years ago, before the building was converted into apartments.
DAVID. And the doors are teak without a nail in them, the rain gutters are lead and the glass in the hall lamps is handblown. You couldn't build this house again for love or money. (*He smiles, slightly modestly.*)
CATHY. My!
DAVID. I've got a diploma that says I'm an achitect, but I've got an obsession that says I'm an actor. I'm going to find out before I give in. I'd starve as an actor but I get all the drafting work I need.
CATHY. Is this your first New York job?
DAVID. Two Off-Off-Broadways, this is my first *single* Off. What about you?

CATHY. Two Offs and one On Broadway.

DAVID. No!

CATHY. Only understudy. We closed in a week. I support *my* obsession by writing free lance book reviews— (*Lifted eyebrows.*) English major—and selling the books I get from the publishers. That's where the real money is. I also write a radio serial. Well, I'm one of the writers.

DAVID. You certainly are industrious.

CATHY. I haven't any choice. I'm supporting this— (*Indicating the room.*) panelling. Champagne appetite, beer pocketbook. My father's saying. Well, before we begin is there anything I can offer you? Milk, tomato juice, yogurt?

DAVID. No, thank you.

CATHY. You can have something alcoholic, if you want it.

DAVID. I don't think we better. We need our wits about us.

CATHY. Yes, we do. (*A moment.*) We have the parts, haven't we? I mean, definitely.

DAVID. My agent thought we had.

CATHY. So did mine, but sometimes they audition people in other places.

DAVID. The director rehearsed us all afternoon.

CATHY. He left a few times. That worries me. Where did he go?

DAVID. Men's room, I hope.

CATHY. (*Solemnly.*) Amen. (*For courage.*) He *was* very complimentary to both of us.

DAVID. In the beginning. He wasn't too happy later.

CATHY. (*Recalling.*) No. He said we were too stiff.

DAVID. No, he said *I* was too stiff.

CATHY. No, he said *we* were playing it stiffly.

DAVID. But *I* was talking, he meant me.

CATHY. *I* was reacting. I could have been reacting stiffly.

DAVID. (*Smile.*) Let's work out the stiffness together. Shall we begin? (*Cathy sits on the couch, he joins her. They open their scripts. During it:*) My suggestion is we read the insurance scene together once, with the stage directions, and then we do it with the physical action. Does that suit you?

CATHY. Fine.

DAVID. I don't want to impose my way of working on you. If you have any objections speak right up. Please.

CATHY. No objections. Fire away.

7

DAVID. (*Back to the script.*) Well, here we go. (NOTE: *David and Cathy should read the parts they are playing as credibly as they can, permitting the mishaps in the repetition to be without distraction. David uses his normal conversational voice when he reads the stage directions and projects as an actor when he reads the lines of the play.*) The stage is deserted. The outer door opens and Stanley enters, speaking before he's closed the door behind him. (*Stage voice.*) Ellen, I'm home! (*Directions voice.*) Ellen enters from kitchen.

CATHY. (*Brightly.*) How was your day, dear?

DAVID. (*Elated.*) I though you'd never ask! Fabulous!

CATHY. Good!

DAVID. (*Directions voice.*) They kiss as befits two healthy, young people in love. He takes Ellen by the hand and moves her onto the couch. (*Stage voice.*) You better sit down, it's that kind of news. (*Directions voice.*) He takes coat off and throws it carelessly on the arm of the couch, sitting beside her.

CATHY. I'm all ears.

DAVID. (*Directions voice.*) The following scene is played at counterpoint. While Stanley is relating his business adventure Ellen becomes progressively romantic. In sequence, she stares at him adoringly, she removes his tie, she puts her hand inside his shirt, finally placing her head on his lap, leading to a passionate embrace. (*Stage voice.*) You remember that fellow Carl Cooper I introduced you to at the Garden a couple of weeks ago? At the hockey game?

CATHY. No, I don't.

DAVID. He was with a red headed girl with a green hat.

CATHY. I remember the hat.

DAVID. Well, out of a clear sky he called me up. He'd never called me before. I've played handball with him and talked with him in the locker room, but that's all. I must've mentioned to him I was with Bundy Insurance because he knew where to call me. "How long are you going to be in your office?" he asked. "I'll be here all afternoon," I said. "Stay right where you are, I'll be up in twenty minutes," he said. I forgot about him. Sure enough twenty minutes later he pops in. "Stanley," he says, "This is your lucky day." "Happy to hear it," I said. "Why?" "Because I just threw my brother-in-law out of my office. He handles the insurance for my three garages. He USED to handle it. You're elected! Do you

8

want it?" Well, I was speechless. But not for long. I rushed him into J.B.'s office, half an hour later we had a drink over a signed contract and you, young lady, are going to get the furriest coat under a thousand bucks you ever saw. They come under a thousand dollars, don't they?

CATHY. (*Lovingly.*) Some do. But I don't need a fur coat, dear.

DAVID. I want you to have a fur coat. You know why? I want you naked in a fur coat. I read that in a book once and it turned me on. You're married to a dirty young man.

CATHY. (*Throatily.*) Well, I hope so.

DAVID. (*Directions voice, throwing the line away.*) They look at each other a long moment and fall into a passionate embrace. The phone rings, etcetera. (*Looks at her.*) Well, that's it. That's the part that made the trouble. (*He gets up, as does she.*) Let's walk through it once. We'll probably have to stop and go, but it'll smooth out. You pop into the kitchen, I'll come through the door. Your cue is, "Ellen, I'm home." (*She nods and goes into the kitchen while David goes out the door, closing it behind him. There is a pause, then we hear the door handle being rattled, since David has locked himself out.*)

CATHY'S VOICE. I don't hear you! (*David knocks on the door.*)

DAVID'S VOICE. It's locked! The door's locked!

CATHY'S VOICE. Louder, I can't hear you! (*We hear the buzzer as David rings the bell. Cathy hurries out of the kitchen.*) Oh, dear! (*She goes quickly to the door, on which David is still rapping and opens it.*)

BOTH. Sorry.

CATHY. It locks by itself.

DAVID. My fault, I should have known.

CATHY. You can start from inside. (*She returns to the kitchen, David to the door. He opens and shuts it loudly.*)

DAVID. Ellen, I'm home! (*Cathy enters.*)

CATHY. How was your day, dear?

DAVID. I thought you'd never ask! Fabulous!

CATHY. Good!

DAVID. (*Reading.*) They kiss as befits two healthy, young people in love. (*They step to each other and quite self-consciously brush lips. We now see the reason for the director's criticism. David refers quickly back to the script. He reads further, in his normal voice.*) He pulls Ellen onto the couch. (*With one hand holding the*

9

script, he takes Ellen by the hand and moves her onto the couch.) You better sit down, it's that kind of news. (Referring back to the script and the stage directions.) He takes coat off and throws it carelessly on the arm of the couch, sitting beside her. (He puts the script down a moment as he quickly sheds his coat and throws it on the couch, sitting beside her.)

CATHY. I'm all ears.

DAVID. (Reading the stage directions in a quick sing song mumble.) The following scene is played at counterpoint. While Stanley is relating his business adventure Ellen becomes progressively romantic. (The next sentence should be heard clearer.) In sequence, she stares at him adoringly, she removes his tie, she puts her hand inside his shirt, finally placing her head on his lap, leading to a passionate embrace. (Now normally.) Well, that's clear enough. Shouldn't be a problem. The ball's in your corner, you know.

CATHY. What do you mean?

DAVID. Well, I only take my reactions from what you do. I'm carrying on with my office talk and I'll change my tone as I become— (He is slightly hesitant.) distracted.

CATHY. (Forcing herself to be at ease.) Yes, of course. All right, here we go. (Repeating.) I'm all ears.

DAVID. (He refers to the script occasionally.) You remember that fellow Carl Cooper I introduced you to at the Garden a couple of weeks ago? At the hockey game?

CATHY. No, I don't.

DAVID. He was with a red headed girl with a green hat.

CATHY. I remember the hat.

DAVID. Well, out of a clear sky he called me up. He'd never called me before. I've played handball with him and talked with him in the locker room, but that's all. I must've mentioned to him I was with Bundy Insurance because he knew where to call me. (About here Cathy withdraws active listening and puts her arm on the couch back, her face in her hand, looking at David adoringly.) "How long are you going to be in your office?" he asked. "I'll be here all afternoon," I said. "Stay where you are, I'll be up in twenty minutes," he said. (Now Cathy reaches over to his tie with one hand and tries to pull it loose and off.) I forgot about him. Sure enough twenty— (Cathy has put her hand between his collar and neck and he chokes during his speech.) twenty minutes later— uck—

CATHY. I'm sorry, I'm choking you. I can't seem to loosen your tie.

DAVID. Mmmm. (*Thinks.*) What I'll do is loosen my collar when I take my coat off. That'll leave room for your fingers. (*He loosens the tie for her.*) How's that? Try it now. (*She does.*) Okay?

CATHY. That's better.

DAVID. Just pull away and it'll come off. (*Cathy does, the tie comes off. She puts it beside her. Back to the script.*) I forgot about him. Sure enough twenty minutes later he pops in. (*Cathy starts to unbutton his shirt. She's having trouble and David helps her by unnaturally facing her while he continues speaking.*) "Stanley," he says, "This is your lucky day." (*Cathy sits up.*) What's the matter?

CATHY. (*Showing him.*) The button's come off. I'm sorry. (*She starts to get up.*) I'll sew it back on.

DAVID. (*Stopping her.*) Don't worry about it.

CATHY. It'll only take a minute.

DAVID. Let's keep going. This is more important. I'll angle around, facing you more. Try unbuttoning my shirt now. (*Cathy carefully puts the button on the couch arm. She now tries to unbutton him, but the position is awkward.*)

CATHY. Oh, dear. (*Showing him.*) Another button. They're not sewed on very strong.

DAVID. Yeah. Well, we can lick that. I'll make the button holes bigger.

CATHY. Yes, that would help. (*She places the second button with the first.*) If you'll bring me a shirt I'll do it. I'm very good with button holes.

DAVID. (*Unbuttoning another two.*) Until then. (*He is now unbuttoned to the navel.*) There you are. (*Back to the script.*) "Stanley, this is your lucky day." "Happy to hear it," I—ouch! (*In sticking her hand into his shirt Cathy has evidently scratched him.*)

CATHY. I scratched you!

DAVID. (*Smiles.*) Well, either I wear an undershirt or you cut your fingernails.

CATHY. I'm awfully sorry. I don't know why I'm so awkward.

DAVID. Let's keep going. Put your hand back. (*She does, not easily. David resumes with the script.*) "Happy to hear it," I said. "Why?" "Because I just threw my brother-in-law out of my office.

He handles the insurance for my three garages. He USED to handle it. You're elected! Do you want it?" Well, I was speechless. (*Cathy has decided this is the moment to lay her head on his lap. David self-consciously spreads himself to give her room. Her head is not on his lap but on his knees. Away from the script.*) Are you comfortable?

CATHY. (*Not true.*) I'm all right. (*They are rigid with unease.*)

DAVID. (*Resuming script.*) Well, I was speechless. But not for long. I rushed him into J.B.'s office, half an hour later we had a drink over a signed contract and you, young lady, are going to get the furriest coat under a thousand bucks you ever saw. They come under a thousand dollars, don't they?

CATHY. Some do. But I don't need a fur coat, dear.

DAVID. (*From the script.*) I want you to have a fur coat. You know why? I want you naked in a fur coat. I read that in a book once and it turned me on. You're married to a dirty young man.

CATHY. Well, I hope so.

DAVID. (*From the script.*) They look at each other a long moment and fall into a passionate embrace. (*They are quite self-conscious. A moment's hesitation and they make a simultaneous lurch at each other. Their noses would have met straight on if they hadn't braked. Cathy inclines her head to the right, but unfortunately so has David. She quickly changes to the left, but so has he. They smile, forced.*) We have to come to a decision here.

CATHY. Yes, we do.

DAVID. A sort of modus operandi. Do you normally kiss left or right?

CATHY. (*Recalling, moving her head both ways.*) I'm not sure. Either way works.

DAVID. People usually incline their heads either right or left. Not counting emergencies.

CATHY. (*Experimenting further.*) You're right. Not counting emergencies I'm left.

DAVID. Well, I'm right. That simplifies it. (*A moment of mutual strained smiling and they join lips, arms around each other, the scripts making the embrace quite awkward. He jerks back, holding the back of his neck.*)

CATHY. What is it?

DAVID. (*Checking if there's blood on his fingers.*) The metal fastener on your script stabbed me. We're not going to get through this rehearsal without Blue Cross.

12

CATHY. (*Tamping down the fastener.*) I can't keep repeating I'm sorry, but I am.

DAVID. It's all right. Well, that's it. Roughly.

CATHY. (*Adjusting herself, hair and skirt.*) Very roughly.

DAVID. Of course we don't know our lines yet. Reading with a script in our hands and co-ordinating the action isn't easy.

CATHY. No, it isn't. We'll fall into it gradually. A little patience. (*A rueful smile.*) Which I hope the director has. (*She gets up.*) Let's take a little breather. (*Takes the two buttons.*) I'll sew your buttons back on if you take your shirt off.

DAVID. No, no, the laundry'll sew them on.

CATHY. (*Giving him the buttons.*) See if I drew blood when I scratched you. The least I can do is supply mercurochrome and a band-aid. (*David looks.*)

DAVID. No blood. As good as new.

CATHY. Would you like a drink now? It might be a good idea. Relax us. (*He is thinking of something, bouncing the butttons in his hand.*) What are you thinking about? Go on, say it. This is the time for it.

DAVID. I was thinking that if we drank the amount of liquor we need to be relaxed—both of us—we'd be too far gone to say the lines.

CATHY. It's my fault.

DAVID. No, it isn't. (*He thinks further. Decides. He takes her by the shoulders and gently seats her back on the couch. She is puzzled at his manner, but submits. He stoops to her.*) I want to speak to you very seriously.

CATHY. Yes?

DAVID. I don't want you to decide anything until you've heard me out completely. Will you agree to that?

CATHY. Agreed. (*He walks and talks, occasionally bouncing the buttons.*)

DAVID. If I asked you to dinner tonight, would you accept?

CATHY. Not tonight. I'm going to do my hair. I need all the help I can get.

DAVID. Would you go out with me tomorrow night?

CATHY. I'm not clear on this. Are you asking me?

DAVID. I'm leading up to something. I'm making a point. If I did ask you, is it possible you'd accept?

CATHY. It's possible.

DAVID. All right. Now. I'd take you to dinner and make a great effort to be charming, and then I'd see you home, and I'd kiss you on the cheek—that's my routine on a first date—and I'd ask you for lunch for the following day. Is it possible you'd go out with me again?

CATHY. (*Puzzled, but amused.*) Possible. If you'd been charming enough.

DAVID. During lunch I'd ask to take you to dinner.

CATHY. Well now!

DAVID. That's my operation. Blitz. Is it conceivable you'd accept?

CATHY. Conceivable. I'm counting you're still charming.

DAVID. On the third date I bring flowers.

CATHY. I like flowers. You're doing fine.

DAVID. May I ask, at the end of the evening, if you'd ask me in for a drink?

CATHY. I might.

DAVID. And we'd end up in bed. (*Cathy doesn't change expression and remains non-committal during David's recital.*) That's par for the course. That's average, that's normal, that's accepted. There have been cases in recorded history where people got in the hay sooner, and maybe one or two cases later, but three dates is standard. Now here's the proposition I offer you, and remember you promised to think about it before you answer. That scene we just did was terrible. And it's possible it was terrible because we're terrible, but I don't want to believe that. What's unfortunate is it calls for two strangers like us to be intimate and familiar and at ease, and we were embarrassed and self-conscious. We weren't just tense, we were rigid! When you put your head in my lap—on the edge of my knees actually—both our voices went up two octaves. I've been hiding something from you. I didn't mean to tell you this because I didn't want you to be nervous. My agent told me we're first choice but they're holding the couple that read after us as standbys. (*He takes a deep breath.*) What I'm proposing, clear and simple, is that we get in bed right now and get it over with so we can play the goddammed scene relaxed! (*He turns away, his hands in his hip pockets, breathing hard out of tension. He turns back to her. She has never taken her eyes off him or changed her expression. Lower, but just as fervent.*) I'm still taking you to dinner, to lunch, to dinner and the flowers. I owe you the respect, the dignity, the courtesy of courtship, I'm only asking you to get in bed retroactively! (*She still says nothing. Earnestly, simply.*) It comes

14

down to simply this. How much do we want the parts? (*Now Cathy looks straight ahead. Another moment and then, not looking down, one foot at a time, she slowly shucks her shoes. David, however, does look at them.*)

CATHY. (*Straight ahead, a faraway voice.*) You're not wrong. No, you're not.

DAVID. (*Grateful.*) You won't regret it. (*She looks at him sharply. He corrects himself hastily.*) I mean we're doing the right thing. (*Cathy gets up, she sighs. She forces a smile.*)

CATHY. You're not going to forget the flowers?

DAVID. (*Sincerely, fervently.*) No, I won't. (*She starts toward the bedroom, taking her blouse off.*)

CATHY. They never mentioned anything about this at Actors Lab. (*He follows.*)

CURTAIN

ACT ONE

SCENE 2

Three weeks later. Eleven A.M.

The apartment now has some additions, all testifying to a male's presence on the premises. They consist of two sneakers, five feet apart, on the floor; a baseball glove on a chair; a man's sweater over the chair's back, and a tie; a baseball cap hung on a light fixture; a putter against the L. wall, with two golf balls beside it. An empty champagne bottle, with a ribbon around its neck, and some used glasses, are on the table. There is a general disarray of chairs and objects which is in contrast to the previous tidy ambiance.

Cathy is lying on the couch, her head on David's lap, reading a book. David is reading, actually rereading, their play review in the New York Times. The most noticeable contrast between the previous scene and this is the intimate position of Cathy and David. David wears a sweat suit and is barefoot. Cathy wears blue jeans, a shirt and moccasins.

The Curtain Rises on a few moments of silence.

DAVID. (*Finally, still reading.*) Move a little. My crotch has fallen asleep.

CATHY. (*Moves her head half an inch. Still reading.*) Crotchety young man. (*They read further. Not looking at him.*) Haven't you memorized that review yet?

DAVID. Not all of it. Just— (*He lowers the paper.*) "David Dillon, in the role of the young husband trapped in the insurance business, was clean and incisive." Good man, Gussow.

CATHY. You hated him yesterday.

DAVID. In art one must be objective. I don't carry grudges.

CATHY. Could it be that you hated him because he didn't mention you the last time he reviewed you and now you're "clean and incisive"?

DAVID. He's matured. The man has learned, that's all. Would you like to hear his comment on you again?

CATHY. (*Putting the book down and reciting from memory.*) "Catherine Temple has an appealing luminous quality. She glows. We should hear from her." (*Strong.*) You will! (*Resumes reading.*) Darling man.

DAVID. Let's look up the word "luminous."

CATHY. (*Reading her book.*) "Shining, emitting, reflecting, or suggesting, light." Webster's Unabridged.

DAVID. Oh, you ham!

CATHY. "Luminous" is better than "incisive." And I "glow" besides.

DAVID. We all came off pretty good except for Crystal.

CATHY. He didn't say anything terrible about Crystal.

DAVID. If he called you "stereotyped" you wouldn't have memorized Webster's. (*Abrupt change.*) What do you want to do now?

CATHY. I have to finish this book, David. It's a definite assignment.

DAVID. (*Groping for her.*) Finish it later.

CATHY. Listen, you go do your jogging and we'll see when you come back.

DAVID. You get tired jogging.

CATHY. (*Disengaging him.*) That's the idea.

16

DAVID. (*Still grabbing.*) Today's special. Let's celebrate. Let's stay in all day and fool around.

CATHY. (*Fighting him off.*) We celebrated last night. (*He's holding something.*) David! Hasn't that champagne worn off?

DAVID. I've just made a milestone medical discovery. There's no aphrodisiac like a good review. (*He's got her down, all right.*) I can't help it, I'm a nymphomaniac.

CATHY. (*Beneath him.*) Only the female can be properly termed a nymphomaniac.

DAVID. (*Through his teeth.*) Quiet, you English major! (*They kiss, holding it.*)

CATHY. (*After a moment. Lower.*) I thought your crotch was asleep. (*And the doorbell buzzes.*)

DAVID. (*Displeased.*) Who dat, dammit?

CATHY. (*Disengaging herself.*) David Merrick. He wants you to get out of your contract and play *Hamlet*.

DAVID. Let him get Laurence Olivier.

CATHY. He won't take second best. (*She starts toward the door, repairing her shirt.*)

DAVID. Why don't people announce themselves from downstairs? So we can turn them down.

CATHY. That's why. (*She opens the door.*) Crystal! Come on in! (*And Crystal enters. The Casting Directory says she's thirty but she's a few years older. She's wise and tough and doesn't remember her original hair color. Heart of gold and bust to match.*)

DAVID. Hello, Crystal!

CRYSTAL. Hi ya, kids. I started to take a long walk but my feet hurt. I haven't interrupted anything?

DAVID. No, we were just glancing at the review.

CRYSTAL. Is it all right?

CATHY. (*Surprised.*) Haven't you read it?

CRYSTAL. I never read reviews. Never. I ignore them.

DAVID. Well, we ought to have a nice little run.

CRYSTAL. I'm glad to hear it.

DAVID. Cathy is "luminous," I'm "clean and incisive."

CRYSTAL. "Clean"? What kind of comment is that? You use a detergent?

DAVID. It means my characterization was clean. Sharp. Finely etched.

CRYSTAL. Why didn't he say so? (*Bitterly.*) "Stereotyped." Hah! Some noun!

CATHY. It's an adjective.

CRYSTAL. (*A look at her.*) I forgot. Miss Book Reviewer. If there's one thing my characterization was not, was stereotyped. (*Pointing to herself.*) I'm living with the director. Harry worked on me every night. He said he was giving me a new dimension and I know he did. I felt it. (*She sits.*)

CATHY. I thought you were very effective.

CRYSTAL. You're damned right I was! (*She reflects. Cathy and David feel for her. They wait.*) You know what may be my trouble?

CATHY. What?

CRYSTAL. This is a small town.

DAVID. New York?

CRYSTAL. I mean show people, they know everybody's business. They know I'm living with the director. From that they jump to the conclusion that I got the job account of him. Then, when they see me in the part they discount my ability.

DAVID. Could be.

CRYSTAL. It's happened to me before. (*She reflects on that. They just look at her. She comes out of her reverie.*) Well, I'm glad for you two.

CATHY. Thank you.

CRYSTAL. Keep your fingers crossed. The movie and TV scouts'll be around this week. (*Cathy and David hold up crossed fingers.*) You know something? When you two were rehearsing the first day I said to my agent "I'll bet you a drink against a dinner they're out tomorrow." And he wouldn't take the bet. You certainly surprised me the next day. You surprised Harry too. (*Cathy and David glance at each other, unnoticed.*)

CATHY. (*Quickly.*) Harry got a very good review, "The direction is original and ingenious."

CRYSTAL. He's got the review pasted over the bathroom mirror so he can see it while he's shaving. He's shaved twice this morning.

DAVID. (*Going to his sneakers.*) That reminds me, I better get more copies. They may run out of newspapers. (*He puts the sneakers on without socks, without lacing them.*)

CRYSTAL. Between you and Harry the *Times'* circulation's going to take a big jump today.

18

DAVID. Back in a minute. (*Cathy watches him leave, Crystal watches Cathy.*)

CRYSTAL. You got a thing going full blast here, haven't you?

CATHY. (*Smiling, nods.*) Uh, huh.

CRYSTAL. Sensational?

CATHY. Uh, huh.

CRYSTAL. Enjoy. Nothing like it. Been there fifty times.

CATHY. Not fifty, Crystal!

CRYSTAL. Who's counting? (*The label on the champagne bottle catches her eye.*) Spanish champagne? Didn't know they made it. Any good?

CATHY. It's slightly cheaper. Tenth the price.

CRYSTAL. (*Fingering the bottle.*) That's for me. I'll sponge the labels off. Anybody I know can't tell the difference. (*She looks the room over, settling on the cap on the lamp. Cathy sees where she's looking.*)

CATHY. David has a lot of wonderful qualities but neatness isn't one of them.

CRYSTAL. Be grateful for the other qualities.

CATHY. I hint, but it doesn't do any good. He's a walking typhoon.

CRYSTAL. You can't train 'em. They're animals.

CATHY. My father is very neat.

CRYSTAL. They come in all models. I've had some neat, some slobs. If you have your choice take the slob every time.

CATHY. (*Amused.*) Really?

CRYSTAL. (*Nods.*) I had a neat one once, drove me crazy. Kept his shorts on hangers. Who saw them? Numbers on his toothbrushes. God forbid he'd use Friday's on Saturday. His teeth'd fall out. We broke up the day he got out of bed in the middle of an affair to turn off the television set. (*Shakes her head, from side to side.*) What the hell do we need men for? (*Pause. She nods.*) I know what we need men for.

CATHY. (*Obliged to say something.*) They're handy.

CRYSTAL. That's one word. I love to sleep with them but I hate to wake up with them. I don't wake up pretty. I scare the hell out of *me!* A man shouldn't see a woman until it's dark. Around six o'clock he should hand her a martini. With two olives.

CATHY. Yes, that would be nice. Even one olive. (*A pause.*)

CRYSTAL. Harry's getting on my nerves.

19

CATHY. Oh, I *am* sorry, Crystal.

CRYSTAL. He's all right, it's me. I haven't very good nerves. I'd like to leave him.

CATHY. Then why don't you?

CRYSTAL. I can't. We're living in my apartment. (*A moment.*) I still don't see how he moved in. They do it gradually. They take you to dinner, they bring you flowers, and you start having an affair. That's the best part, the beginning. For a while they get out of bed and go home. Then, one day after a big night, they sleep over. So they use your shaving your legs razor. Then you go out formal and he can't put on a tuxedo in the morning so he brings over a change of clothes. Soon he's got half the closet! (*She cocks an eye.*) I've given this a lot of thought. What's the exact step that starts you living together? And I think I've got it. It's when they ask you to pick up their cleaning. (*She nods.*) That's it. Three times I've picked up the cleaning and three times they've moved in. Oh, they pay half the expenses, and it seems like a practical idea when you talk it over, but it really isn't. You're now cook, bed-mate and towel picker up after. You're a wife without community property, that's all. What the hell did we really get out of women's lib? We're free women. We're giving it away free! I've got a hunch we're going to wake up one morning and find out that women's lib was started by a man. Those louses are capable of it. They probably met in some bowling alley and figured it out. They're hysterical laughing. (*A moment.*) How did David move in here?

CATHY. I picked up his cleaning.

CRYSTAL. Figures. (*Pause.*) I heard your soap opera on the radio. (*Shakes her head.*) Wild.

CATHY. (*Smiles defensively.*) It's not written for you, Crystal.

CRYSTAL. Marylou's pregnant, she doesn't know who the father is, her dog got run over and she's getting a rash. Who is it written for?

CATHY. For hard working house wives.

CRYSTAL. Why?

CATHY. To make them feel better by contrast.

CRYSTAL. How's Marylou going to get out of that mess?

CATHY. I haven't the faintest idea.

CRYSTAL. You haven't?

CATHY. I'll think of something. Don't worry about her.

CRYSTAL. You've got a hell of an imagination.

CATHY. It's just a knack. I think it comes from being an only child. You invent things to entertain yourself. I like inventing. (*Pause.*)

CRYSTAL. Harry's cheating on me.

CATHY. How do you know?

CRYSTAL. Woman's intuition. I caught him.

CATHY. What did he say?

CRYSTAL. "Ouch," I hit him with a ketchup bottle. You couldn't tell the blood from the ketchup.

CATHY. Aren't you going to do anything about it?

CRYSTAL. Well, he had a pretty good excuse.

CATHY. I'd like to hear it!

CRYSTAL. It was with his ex-wife. He owes her back alimony. It was that or go to jail.

CATHY. I'd've let him go to jail!

CRYSTAL. He owed her nine hundred dollars. We haven't got that much. He said he did it for me.

CATHY. (*Flabbergasted.*) Of all the gall!

CRYSTAL. Oh, ex-wife, I can see that. Old times. I wouldn't stand for a new one.

CATHY. You certainly are tolerant, Crystal.

CRYSTAL. (*Carefully.*) You wouldn't have stood for it?

CATHY. I would not!

CRYSTAL. You'd leave him?

CATHY. (*Firm.*) Like a shot! Let me tell you something, Crystal! I accept this modern living together, it's part of our mores—

CRYSTAL. Our what?

CATHY. Our conventions! But the very act of living outside of wedlock imposes an even stricter morality on the man and the woman! Infidelity between lovers is outside the pale! Unforgiveable!

CRYSTAL. (*Admiringly.*) You talk like a book reviewer.

CATHY. (*Right on.*) You're humiliating yourself! *That's* what women's lib is about! Self respect! For your body and your pride! You leave him!

CRYSTAL. You'd leave David?

CATHY. Of course I would!

CRYSTAL. What about that—sensational? 'T'ain't easy to come by.

CATHY. (*Deliberately.*) It wouldn't be sensational any more! I—don't believe—in—overlapping!

CRYSTAL. Overlapping?

CATHY. One lover at a time! For him and for me! It may be a fine point to you, Crystal, meaning no offense, but that's my morality, as little as it is, and I cling to it!

CRYSTAL. (*Carefully.*) But if you had your druthers, you'd rather never hear about it?

CATHY. Indeed I would want to hear about it, and if you ever have the faintest suspicion of David wandering I'd be very grateful, as a friend and sister Equity member, if you came right to me and told me about it!

CRYSTAL. (*A long pause, while Crystal makes up her mind. Sadly.*) Well, you asked for it.

CATHY. (*Puzzled.*) Asked for what?

CRYSTAL. (*Pause.*) Your boy's wandering.

CATHY. (*Thrown.*) What do you mean by "wandering"?

CRYSTAL. What do you think I mean by "wandering"?

CATHY. You're not saying anything specific. If you've seen him talking to another girl, doing his charm act—

CRYSTAL. (*Interrupting.*) I'm not talking about talking.

CATHY. (*Disturbed, but making an effort to conceal it.*) You're implying he's having an affair elsewhere?

CRYSTAL. I'm implying.

CATHY. Frankly, I don't believe you.

CRYSTAL. (*Sadly.*) We always say that. We don't want to believe.

CATHY. (*Slightly angry.*) There's no way he could be having an affair! I'm with him day and night! Except for twenty-five minutes in the second act he's never out of my sight!

CRYSTAL. (*Quietly.*) That's when.

CATHY. He's in his dressing room then!

CRYSTAL. (*Same tone.*) That's where.

CATHY. (*Lost.*) With whom?

CRYSTAL. One of those N.Y.U. drama school kids that thinks actors are glamorous. She had her school books with her.

CATHY. How do you know?

CRYSTAL. I'm off-stage in the second act. I was leaving the john the first time I saw her leaving his dressing-room. Kissing and hugging goodbye. The second time I listened. She came out crying.

He may have her in a jam. (*Cathy can just stare, her unhappiness too revealed.*) I usually keep my big fat yap shut in things like this, and if you were a little tougher broad I would have, but you look like you bleed easy. Take it from Crystal, who's been there, it hurts less now than it would later.

CATHY. (*Controlling herself.*) I'm happy you told me, Crystal.

CRYSTAL. No, you're not. Not now. You will be later. Can an old battle scarred veteran make a suggestion?

CATHY. (*Tight lipped.*) What sort of suggestion?

CRYSTAL. Don't do anything until you cool off. And then don't do anything. He's only a man and a man's half a tom cat. You know the score now, use him the way he's using you. You're having laughs, aren't you? Keep laughing. That's a kind of women's lib bit, the way I look at it.

CATHY. You mean keep going to bed with him?

CRYSTAL. You're so crude.

CATHY. I wouldn't let him put a finger on me if I was to burn at the stake!

CRYSTAL. (*Deliberate non-sequitur.*) I saw Ingrid Bergman in that. She was great.

CATHY. He'll be out of here today!

CRYSTAL. It's not so easy, they don't go that quick. They swear they won't anymore, they plead, they cry. Real tears sometimes. (*Smiles, recalling.*) Forgiving 'em is fun. Do it slow, make it last.

CATHY. He'll be out of this apartment today!

CRYSTAL. Want to bet?

CATHY. You name it!

CRYSTAL. Bottle of scotch?

CATHY. You're on.

CRYSTAL. Not Spanish, eh? Johnny Walker.

CATHY. Johnny Walker. I'll phone you as soon as he's out.

CRYSTAL. Well, I can't lose. If you manage it, tell me how, I'll use it on Harry. (*Thinks.*) Of course I could just leave Harry with the apartment. We owe two months rent. Serve him right. And I know where *I* could go. There's some guy who wants to keep me. (*Nose crinkling.*) He's a little old for real laughs, you know what I mean, but it's something to think about. I went that route once. Comfortable. Apartment paid for, little charge accounts here and there, but it was nerve wracking. He had his own key. You can't ask a guy who's paying for an apartment not to have a key. You're always looking over your shoulder. (*Thinks about it.*) Well, not really over your shoulder. (*Thinks further.*) Could be though. You get the picture. (*The door opens and David enters, carrying five copies of the New York* Times.)

DAVID. Anything happen while I was gone?

CRYSTAL. We baked a cake.

DAVID. My agent didn't call?

CRYSTAL. Just Metro-Goldwyn-Mayer and Paramount. We hung up. (*She gets up.*) Well, I'll be moseying along.

DAVID. Glad you dropped in, Crystal.

CRYSTAL. (*At the door, to him.*) I try to do one good deed a day. See you at the theatre, you lovely people. (*And she's out. Cathy has been looking at David with narrowed eyes from the moment he entered.*)

DAVID. Thought she'd never leave. Lucky I got to the newsstand in time. They only had five papers left. (*He puts them down.*) How many do you need, Cath?

CATHY. (*Flat.*) The one I bought'll do.

DAVID. You need one to send your folks and one for your scrap-book. I'll keep the other four. (*He goes to the notebook on the bar and will bring it back to the table.*) Before I forget. (*He opens the book, takes the pencil clipped on it, and starts to write.*) Five *Timeses*. Wait a minute, six, you paid for the first. (*Corrects.*) Four on my account, two yours. Do you think I've forgotten anything lately?

CATHY. No, I don't.

DAVID. Sometimes *you* forget. (*The champagne bottle before him catches his eye.*) The champagne! Did you enter it? (*He looks.*) No, you didn't. We have to watch that, Cathy, no cheating! How much was it?

CATHY. I contributed it.

DAVID. Nothing doing! That's a mutual item. We've had this out. How much was it? I insist?

CATHY. Two dollars and fifty cents.

DAVID. (*Entering it.*) Two dollars and fifty cents.

CATHY. (*Deliberately.*) Plus the tax.

DAVID. How much was the tax?

CATHY. I don't remember. Why don't you call up and find out?

DAVID. (*Weighs this. Decides against it.*) The phone call'd be more than the tax. Make it a dime. Two sixty.

CATHY. That's fair.

DAVID. Can you think of anything else you've forgotten?

CATHY. I just remembered I forgot to enter your cleaning.

DAVID. (*Looking for it on the previous two pages.*) You did? (*Can't find the item. Cheerful enough.*) That's right, it's not here. How much was it?

CATHY. Four dollars.

DAVID. (*Entering it.*) Even?

CATHY. Even. (*He clips the pencil back onto the notebook and brings it back to the bar, talking.*)

DAVID. Well, this is a great day!

CATHY. So far. (*David kicks off his sneakers. Cathy watches him do it.*) Put your sneakers back on. (*He comes to her, behind her, and kisses the top of her head.*)

DAVID. (*Romantically.*) They'll only have to come off again. Needless duplication of labor.

CATHY. Not now.

DAVID. Mood's gone, huh?

CATHY. That's right.

DAVID. You know why?

CATHY. Why?

DAVID. Empty stomach. Your metabolism's low. Why don't you cook us up a hell of a brunch? What've you got?

CATHY. Hemlock. (*He has been nuzzling her hair and hasn't caught the word.*)

DAVID. Ham hock?

CATHY. Hemlock?

DAVID. I don't get it.

CATHY. You will.

DAVID. You're in one of your Noel Coward moods, aren't you? One liners. The first play I ever did was *Private Lives*. In High School.

CATHY. That must have been something.

DAVID. No, the girl wasn't very good. And the principal took out the sexy lines. Instead of going to bed they played backgammon. It didn't make sense.

CATHY. It makes sense. (*The downstairs' buzzer sounds, from its speaker hole, next to the door.*)

DAVID. No, not somebody else! We're living in Grand Central Terminal! (*She gets up and goes to it.*) Don't let 'em up, no matter who it is! A man's home is his castle! (*Loud.*) Privacy, dammit!

CATHY. (*Having reached it and pressed the answering button.*) Yes, who is it?

VOICE ON SPEAKER. (*Cheerful.*) This is the garbage man! Do you want any? (*Cathy instantly claps her hand over the hole.*)

CATHY. Oh, my God!

DAVID. Who is it?

CATHY. It's my father!

DAVID. (*Leaping up.*) Your father!

VOICE ON SPEAKER. Cathy! Catherine! Are you there? Do you hear me?

CATHY. (*Floundering.*) Hello, Dad. How are you? (*Anything.*) How've you been?

VOICE ON SPEAKER. (*Puzzled.*) I'm fine, Cathy. Can I come up?

CATHY. Listen, Dad! Give me five minutes! Just five minutes! Walk around the block, will you!

VOICE ON SPEAKER. All right, Cathy. (*The speaker clicks off. Cathy whirls around.*)

CATHY. You get out! Quick! Now!

DAVID. (*Looks down at his jogging suit.*) Like this?

CATHY. Like that! Jog right by him! (*She sees his things.*) And take your putter! I don't play golf!

DAVID. Stick it in the closet!

CATHY. (*Realizing.*) Oh no! You take everything out of the closet! And the bathroom! My father's staying over!

DAVID. Holy mackeral!

CATHY. Hurry!

DAVID. (*Running into the bedroom.*) I'm hurrying! (*Cathy looks the place over. First, she gathers the sweater, the baseball glove and tie, and runs into the bedroom with them. Exiting, she grabs the champagne bottle and the glasses and hurries them behind the bar. She sees the baseball cap on the lamp and takes that, holding it. She thinks. She is looking off in the horizon. Something has occurred to her. She walks slowly toward the chair at the table. She sits, her mind racing. She is reviewing something, mouthing the words. Her head goes from side to side. She nods.*)

DAVID'S VOICE. Where are my pajamas? What did you do with

them? (*Found.*) I got 'em! I got 'em! (*Pause.*) Where are the bottoms? (*Cathy still is reviewing, David appears, breathing hard, carrying a suitcase from which a coat sleeve and a shirt tail dangle. He hurries to his sneakers, putting them on while he speaks.*)

DAVID. Clean as a whistle! What do I do if he isn't walking around the block, if he's in the hall? It'll look funny jogging by him with a suitcase! (*He thinks and answers himself.*) How does he know where I've come from? There are other apartments! I'll walk nonchanlantly past him! (*Another thought.*) Listen, how long will he be here?

CATHY. (*Still mulling.*) I don't know.

DAVID. If it's only a day I can move in with my cousin, but if it's longer I better get a room.

CATHY. (*Still thinking.*) Get a room. He may stay a long time. (*He spies the putter.*)

DAVID. Almost forgot! (*He runs to get the putter. Puts the two golf balls in his pocket.*)

CATHY. (*Subdued.*) Sit down, David.

DAVID. (*Surprised.*) Sit down?

CATHY. Sit down. This'll only take a minute. (*Her tone is that strange that he sits, watching her.*) I've got a confession to make. (*Pause.*) That man's not my father.

DAVID. He's not? (*He recalls.*) You called him "Dad."

CATHY. It's a joke between us. Once he called himself my "sugar daddy," and I've called him "Dad" ever since. He's older than I am. (*A pause.*) He's keeping me.

DAVID. Keeping you?

CATHY. (*She nods reluctantly.*) He pays for this apartment. And little charge accounts.

DAVID. (*Bewildered.*) How long has this been going on?

CATHY. Years.

DAVID. Where has he been these last three weeks?

CATHY. Out of town. (*She's a marvelous liar when she puts her mind to it.*) He wasn't supposed to come back until next week. I wasn't going to tell you until then. I wanted to put it off as long as I could. For the good of the play, and it was—fun. You better go now. (*He picks up his suitcase and starts to the door, dazed. She takes the putter and follows him. She can't suppress a small smile of satisfaction.*) I haven't made you unhappy, have I?

DAVID. (*Some manhood left.*) I'm all right.

27

CATHY. We'll always be friends. I hope.

DAVID. Of course.

CATHY. You're not angry, are you? (*He is.*) You are! I'm surprised. I wouldn't behave this way if I stumbled on you and another girl.

DAVID. You wouldn't stumble on me! I haven't got another girl!

CATHY. Come now, David. The whole last three weeks? Not one little adventure?

DAVID. (*Indignant.*) Certainly not! I never thought of any adventures!

CATHY. (*Looking at him carefully.*) You may be a better actor than I think you are. Run along now. (*She puts the baseball cap on his head, not too straight. He opens the door.*) Don't forget your putter. (*She hands it to him. He lets it dangle dangerously near his feet.*) I'll see you at the theatre tonight. Give a good performance. The show must go on, you know. (*He goes through the door, she closes it behind him. She smiles in grim satisfaction. There is a loud tumbling noise from the stairs. Alarmed, she opens the door, exiting, to investigate.*)

CATHY'S VOICE. Are you all right?

DAVID'S VOICE. I'm all right. (*Cathy reappears, closes the door. She straightens things, reaching the couch, where she spies something we do not see. She reaches down and pulls the pajama bottoms from under the stuffed pad. She hastily lifts the other two pads on the couch. Nothing. She hurries into the bedroom, we hear an off-scene drawer closing. Cathy reappears. She goes to the telephone, looks at the address pad, and dials.*)

CATHY. Harry, Cathy . . . Yes, it *was* a good notice, wasn't it? . . . Thank you for all the patience you had directing me. I may have mentioned it before but after the review it's more sincere . . . Listen, I know Crystal isn't there yet, she only left *here* a few minutes ago, but I want to leave a message for her. The message is "Johnny Walker" . . . Yes, that's the whole message. It's code, she'll know what it means . . . (*There is the buzzer from the door.*) I have to run now, Harry, there's someone at my door. See you tonight. (*She hangs up and goes to the door. She opens it, admitting a handsome, impressive man whose erect carriage reflects his lifetime in the military. Colonel Temple is in his late forties. He wears well tailored civilian clothes and carries a suitcase and David's putter. He puts the bag down, holds out his arms, and Cathy falls in.*) Oh, Dad! It's good to see you!

28

TEMPLE. How's my best girl? (*They break from the embrace and Temple turns to close the door. Only now does Cathy see the putter.*)

CATHY. Where did you get that putter?

TEMPLE. I found it on the stairs. Someone must've dropped it.

CATHY. (*She takes it.*) Probably belongs to a tenant in the building. I'll ask around. (*Stands it against the wall.*) I'm sorry about making you wait but I had a girl friend sleeping over and she was naked as a jay bird. I thought she was going to take a shower but she was in a hurry. You didn't see her, did you?

TEMPLE. No, I didn't. (*She takes him by the hand to the couch.*)

CATHY. Come on, tell me everything! How's mother? How did you leave her?

TEMPLE. Kicking and screaming. She wanted to come along, and I hinted to General Evans, but *his* wife wasn't going, so no luck.

CATHY. Ah, too bad. How long can you stay?

TEMPLE. One night, Cath. I have to be at the Pentagon tomorrow.

CATHY. Oh no!

TEMPLE. I only got here because I told General Evans about your being in the play and he insisted I stop off. How did it go last night?

CATHY. Just marvelous! We have a smash review and we're going to have a nice run. You'll see it tonight.

TEMPLE. I can't wait.

CATHY. I'm "luminous." That's what the *Times* said I was.

TEMPLE. They're not wrong.

CATHY. I wish you'd been here for the opening.

TEMPLE. I almost was. We left Hawaii early enough but when we landed in San Diego we were invited to a Navy seminar, and General Evans thought we'd be rude if we didn't stay over and, well, Colonels don't tell Generals what to do, which is a pity, so I couldn't surprise you.

CATHY. (*For herself.*) Oh, you surprised me. Tell me more about mother!

TEMPLE. She's still—mother. For our anniversary she bought us his and her surf boards.

CATHY. Mother's on a surf board?

TEMPLE. Occasionally. She falls off a lot. She'll never change. She says she's not a grandmother yet. Which brings up, what are prospects?

CATHY. Prospects?

29

TEMPLE. I need a grandson for the West Point football team. Relatives get better seats. Any beaus you fancy particularly?

CATHY. Oh, I had one recently. Very recently.

TEMPLE. How did he get away?

CATHY. I chased him. You know my problem, don't you?

TEMPLE. No, I don't.

CATHY. I have a father fixation. I may end up a spinster.

TEMPLE. I hope not!

CATHY. Don't be alarmed. I have a normal sex drive.

TEMPLE. Wash your mouth with soap.

CATHY. I like to shock you.

TEMPLE. You don't shock me, love. There are areas fathers and daughters should avoid.

CATHY. (*Lovingly.*) You're innocent.

TEMPLE. I'll tell mother. (*He looks at her fondly.*) You're happy, Cath? (*She nods.*) Haven't got it out of your system? (*She shakes her head.*) Don't want to come home?

CATHY. You said I could have two years.

TEMPLE. I was hoping the first year'd be enough.

CATHY. One more year, dad. Let me see if I can make it.

TEMPLE. We miss you.

CATHY. And I miss you. What would you like to do today? Anything special?

TEMPLE. (*Smiles at her.*) Being with you is special, Cathy. (*She looks at him a moment, touched, and leans over and kisses his cheek.*)

CATHY. I do have a father fixation.

TEMPLE. How about my taking you to Pearl's for lunch? You like Chinese food.

CATHY. Pearl's! Oh boy! Can we get in?

TEMPLE. I knew her in Shanghai. When I was a Lieutenant.

CATHY. We can get in.

TEMPLE. (*Getting up.*) Let me wash up.

CATHY. I don't eat before the performance so have a big lunch. Will you be able to hold out until after the theatre?

TEMPLE. I'll manage. I'll make a reservation at the Rainbow Room for supper.

CATHY. (*Beaming.*) Spoil me.

TEMPLE. Except for mother, you're the best dancer I know.

CATHY. Well, look who taught me. (*He starts toward the bedroom door, stops, and turns around.*)

TEMPLE. Would you like to bring someone? I wouldn't mind.
CATHY. No.
TEMPLE. What about your girl friend?
CATHY. (*Forgotten already.*) What girl friend?
TEMPLE. The one who passed me on the stairs wearing a baseball cap. (*He looks at her steadily a long moment and continues into the bedroom. Cathy screws up her face in a funny, frustrated grimace. She really would have liked not to be caught.*)

CURTAIN

ACT ONE

SCENE 3

The following morning. Nine A.M. Cathy, now in a dress, is returning the bed to its couch condition. There are breakfast things on the table. Temple's suitcase is near the door. She works expertly for a while, finishing as Temple enters from the bedroom, buttoning his coat.

CATHY. More coffee, dad?
TEMPLE. I've had three cups, dear. I wish you'd teach mother how to make it.
CATHY. Mother says you've had bad Army coffee all your life and you don't know good coffee when you get it.
TEMPLE. Probably so. (*Catches himself.*) That didn't come out right. I'll take half a cup. (*Cathy will pour while he sits.*)
CATHY. (*Pouring.*) Three quarters?
TEMPLE. No, just half, please. We're scheduled to listen to a Senator this morning and it'll keep me awake.
CATHY. Can you come back here after Washington?
TEMPLE. I don't know, Cath. Our Pentagon business is a little complicated.
CATHY. (*Sitting.*) Important?
TEMPLE. Uh huh.
CATHY. Military secret?
TEMPLE. Uh huh.
CATHY. (*Not serious, their game.*) You can tell me.
TEMPLE. You won't tell anyone?

CATHY. Promise.

TEMPLE. (*Solemnly.*) We're thinking of changing the saluting to the *left* hand.

CATHY. Since I've been a little girl you've never failed to give me a new crazy answer.

TEMPLE. What you didn't know is that some of the answers I gave you were on the level.

CATHY. Oh dear. Dad, thank you for yesterday. It was wonderful.

TEMPLE. I was the one who had the good time, Cathy. (*She looks at him steadily. He sips.*)

CATHY. Well?

TEMPLE. Well what, dear?

CATHY. Aren't you going to ask me about the fellow in the baseball cap?

TEMPLE. No.

CATHY. You're a remarkable father. How do you restrain yourself?

TEMPLE. Wait 'till you're a father. But as long as *you* brought it up. He's not a baseball player, is he?

CATHY. He's an actor! Didn't you recognize him? He plays opposite me!

TEMPLE. I didn't see anyone else on the stage. I consider you gave a solo performance. (*And he suddenly recalls.*) He played the young insurance man?

CATHY. Yes!

TEMPLE. My God, he's an awful actor!

CATHY. He didn't give his usual performance last night.

TEMPLE. Why, he couldn't even remember his lines. And he kept knocking things over.

CATHY. He was upset. Something happened to him.

TEMPLE. (*Doubtfully.*) Well, any son-in-law you bring home is welcome, no matter what he does, but it would be nice if he was good at it.

CATHY. This one won't be a son-in-law. Not a chance.

TEMPLE. That helps. (*A self conscious moment.*)

CATHY. Will you mention him to mother?

TEMPLE. Do you want me to mention it?

CATHY. No.

TEMPLE. Then I won't.

CATHY. Are you embarrassed that I talk about it?

TEMPLE. Yes.

CATHY. Why?

TEMPLE. All fathers are embarrassed.

CATHY. Then how are you so tolerant about it?

TEMPLE. (*A new tone. A sad smile.*) What choice have I?

CATHY. (*Understanding.*) I'm sorry you saw him.

TEMPLE. So am I. (*Cathy is quite unhappy.*) I don't love you any less. You're a different generation, that's all. Very different. (*A moment.*) And I'm not sure you're wrong. (*He gets up, as does she.*) I'll call you from Washington. (*He picks up his suitcase. Wry smile.*) Don't mention that to mother. My not being sure you're wrong.

CATHY. I won't. And thank you. (*Grateful.*) You're my favorite father. (*She kisses him. He opens the door.*)

TEMPLE. Take care, sugar.

CATHY. You too. (*And he's out. She looks at the door a moment, sighs, and turns back to the breakfast dishes. She gathers them on the tray. She puts the tray on a chair and folds the table cloth, putting it over her arm. She picks up the tray and goes into the kitchen. A few moments and the door opens, uncertainly. David enters, with a key. He is quite disheveled and slightly unsteady. He closes the door, still holding the key in his fingers. Cathy comes out of the kitchen, doesn't see him directly, and when she does she emits a tiny, frightened scream. Indignant.*) How did you get in here?

DAVID. (*Weakly.*) With the key. (*She goes to him.*)

CATHY. Give it to me! You don't need it any more! (*He holds it up and she takes it.*) How dare you come in like this? What if my— (*Finds the word.*) friend was here?

DAVID. I waited until he left. He took a taxi. (*Only now has Cathy taken a good look at him.*)

CATHY. What's the matter with you? You look terrible!

DAVID. I feel terrible. I've had an awful time, Cathy.

CATHY. Have you been drinking?

DAVID. Not one drink. (*He sneezes.*)

CATHY. You've got a cold!

DAVID. Don't come near me. I don't want you to catch it.

CATHY. You're going to give a fine performance tonight! As good as last night!

33

DAVID. (*Tottering toward the couch.*) I have to sit down. (*He slumps onto the couch, his head in his hands.*)

CATHY. You didn't remember two consecutive lines! Harry was prompting you so loudly from the wings the audience thought I was acting with *him!*

DAVID. I haven't had one hour's sleep. Maybe an hour and a half. No more. (*He sneezes again.*)

CATHY. How did you get that cold?

DAVID. It was raining, I couldn't get a cab to get to the theatre, and my cousin let me take his car. It's a 1960 convertible and it leaks. I was driving in a bath tub.

CATHY. I thought you felt damp in one scene.

DAVID. It took me half the first act before I picked out your friend. I pegged two wrong fellows before I caught on it was the one applauding your crying scene. Nobody ever applauded there before. I was curious to see him.

CATHY. I hope your curiosity's satisfied!

DAVID. I'm satisfied if you are.

CATHY. I'm satisfied! Would you please go home now and take some aspirin and get in bed?

DAVID. I can't get in bed. My cousin's gone to work and I haven't a key. And I can't call him because he's a telephone repair man. He moves around. I haven't even a suitcase to check into a hotel.

CATHY. (*Impatient with him.*) Then why did you stay out all night?

DAVID. Account of you.

CATHY. On account of me?

DAVID. (*His only show of energy.*) Yes, account of you! You said we're friends, didn't you? I'm worried about you! That's what friends are for! (*She starts to sit on the couch.*) Don't sit near me, you'll catch my cold. (*She goes to the chair, moves it to within five feet and sits.*) Move aside, I don't want to sneeze in your direction. I read that cold germs travel twenty feet.

CATHY. No one's ever been able to identify a cold germ!

DAVID. The *Reader's Digest* has. (*She moves to one side, now facing three quarters front.*)

CATHY. (*Arms folded.*) Well? How did I keep you out all night?

DAVID. I followed you to the Rainbow Room.

CATHY. (*Outraged.*) You what?

DAVID. I sat at the bar. I wanted to size him up. You ate lobster.

CATHY. Well, you have your nerve!

DAVID. What does he do for a living? Is he an Arthur Murray dance instructor?

CATHY. No, he isn't!

DAVID. He dances like a gigolo!

CATHY. (*Pointedly.*) *He* never took anything from a woman in his life!

DAVID. (*Lost on him.*) Then I followed you home. In my bath tub. I waited for him to leave, I wanted to talk to you. But with all the drinks I had at the bar—I had to drink to stay there—I fell asleep in the car.

CATHY. I thought you said you didn't have a drink.

DAVID. I didn't mean last night. And while I was asleep—I must've slipped down—they towed my car away with me in it. I didn't know this was a tow away zone. I had the damnedest time at the police station.

CATHY. The police station!

DAVID. They'd never towed a car away with anyone in it before. They wanted a ruling from the sergeant.

CATHY. (*Fascinated in spite of herself.*) What did they decide?

DAVID. They let me off. I told them my girl was with another man—

CATHY. I'm not your girl! (*Fiercely.*) Did you mention my name?

DAVID. (*Evidently he did.*) Not exactly, but I told them about the play. They can put two and two together if they go see it, but I don't think they're theatre goers. (*To reassure her.*) Anyway, they know the whole plot. (*This might please her.*) They thought it ought to run a long time.

CATHY. (*She eyes this idiot.*) And then what did you do?

DAVID. I came back here and sat in the car across the street and waited for your friend to leave. I had a good look at him. Cathy, he's almost old enough to be your father.

CATHY. He *is* old enough to be my father!

DAVID. I'm trying to help you, Cathy.

CATHY. Don't help me.

DAVID. Having a couple of affairs doesn't make you sophisticated.

CATHY. I've had more than a couple.

DAVID. You told me you had two!

CATHY. I lied!

DAVID. And that makes you a worldly girl?

CATHY. Don't forget I read a lot!

DAVID. He's a married man, isn't he?

CATHY. Yes, he is.

DAVID. You're in a cheap love triangle.

CATHY. Not so cheap. This apartment's expensive.

DAVID. There's the unwritten law. The wife could shoot you. She'd get off scot free.

CATHY. (*Now enjoying herself.*) Oh, she wouldn't do that. I know her.

DAVID. You know her?

CATHY. (*Nods.*) It's a sad story. She's an invalid. Got hurt on a surf board.

DAVID. Does she know about you two?

CATHY. Know what?

DAVID. That he likes you?

CATHY. She knows that. She accepts it.

DAVID. That's sick!

CATHY. That's life. You're the one who's not worldly.

DAVID. How long have you had this relationship?

CATHY. His liking me? Oh, a long time. He put me through college.

DAVID. It started then?

CATHY. Earlier.

DAVID. The man's a mucker!

CATHY. (*Astounded.*) A what?

DAVID. A mucker!

CATHY. That's the first time that word's been uttered in this century! You shouldn't have left the architect business!

DAVID. I haven't left the architect business!

CATHY. Don't throw your drawing board away!

DAVID. I'm beginning to think there may be a different morality among architects!

CATHY. (*Eyes him a moment.*) What about Stanford White?

DAVID. Who?

CATHY. Haven't you ever heard of him?

DAVID. Stanford White? (*Thinks, recalls.*) We had something about him in school. I remember. He built Madison Square Garden.

CATHY. He was *shot* in Madison Square Garden! On the roof!

DAVID. My God, when did that happen?

CATHY. Early this morning. (*She gets up.*) I'm going to give you a hot toddy, and you go into the bedroom and go to sleep. (*She starts into the kitchen.*)

DAVID. (*Leaning back on the couch.*) Thank you, Cath.

CATHY'S VOICE. I'm not doing it for you. I don't want to be playing my scenes with Harry in the wings again.

DAVID. What's the end of it going to be, Cathy?

CATHY'S VOICE. (*Over the running faucet and kettle noise.*) End of what?

DAVID. (*Sleepy voice.*) This unhealthy liaison.

CATHY'S VOICE. What?

DAVID. This unhealthy liaison!

CATHY'S VOICE. Oh, it'll peter out!

DAVID. He's robbing you of your youth!

CATHY'S VOICE. I've got some time to go!

DAVID. You're not even doing him a favor! (*Cathy exits from the kitchen.*)

CATHY. Now that's an insult. (*At the bar.*) The water's heating. (*She will pour a jigger of rum.*)

DAVID. (*Weaker voice.*) The kindest thing you could do is to break it off. (*Now playing a scene for herself during the rum pouring.*)

CATHY. (*Slightly overdone.*) I couldn't be that cruel. He worships me. (*David has closed his eyes.*) He couldn't go on without me. He says the only thing that sustains him in this vale of tears is knowing I'm here—waiting. (*David is asleep.*) He's too fine, too decent, to be hurt. Yes, decent. He's the most selfless, considerate— (*Evidently David snores, because the bzzzz stops Cathy. A reproach.*) I was just warming up. (*She leaves the jigger of rum on the bar and goes to him. She surveys him.*) You missed a great scene, Buster. (*She shakes him by the chin with two fingers, gently.*) Wakey wakey, David. Open your eyes. (*He opens his eyes.*)

DAVID. What is it?

CATHY. You dropped off.

DAVID. I wasn't asleep.

CATHY. (*Helping him up.*) No, but you were snoring.

DAVID. I don't snore.

CATHY. (*Steering him by the arm to the bedroom.*) We had this out once. I played you back a tape recording.

DAVID. That wasn't me. You did something to the tape.

CATHY. You go beddie bye. I'll wake you up later.

DAVID. I'm much obliged, Cathy. (*She watches him walk the rest of the distance to the bedroom.*)

CATHY. (*During the cross.*) Don't sleep on your back! (*From the kitchen comes the sound of the kettle whistling. She goes to it as David closes the bedroom door behind him. She comes out with the kettle and places it on a pad. She takes a large martini shaker from the shelf and pours the glass of rum in it. She appraises it. In that big a container it doesn't seem much. She takes the rum bottle and pours twice the amount in it. Now she pours the hot water. She stirs the contents. She picks it up and would start toward the bedroom, but the doorbell buzzes. Undecided for a moment, a glance to the bedroom door, and then she puts the shaker down on the bar and goes to the door. She opens it and Crystal enters, carrying a paper bag from which she extracts a bottle of* Johnny Walker *scotch.*) What are you doing up this early?

CRYSTAL. (*Going to the bar and depositing it.*) Sleep walking. Fast pay makes fast friends. I went with a bookmaker once who had that printed on his cards. (*She crumples the bag. She stares at the hot toddy. She picks it up and smells it.*) A morning belter! (*Facing her.*) You certainly fooled me.

CATHY. It's medicine.

CRYSTAL. This is your Aunt Crystal! It's *Bacardi* rum! You keep doing this you'll be a character actress in no time!

CATHY. I may have caught David's cold and I'm trying to ward it off!

CRYSTAL. (*She accepts that, looks at the glass again, and brings it over to the table, where she sits.*) Oh. Start warding.

CATHY. (*A look at the bedroom door.*) You could have brought the bottle to the theatre.

CRYSTAL. I did, but you ran out of the place like it was on fire! What was your hurry?

CATHY. (*Going to the chair.*) I had a date.

CRYSTAL. I thought you were afraid the audience was going to come up and get you. That's what I was afraid of. Some performance we gave. What the hell was the matter with David?

38

CATHY. He wasn't himself.

CRYSTAL. If Harry'd caught him he wouldn't have been! Lucky *he* ran, too! Was your date with him?

CATHY. No. Someone else.

CRYSTAL. That's pretty quick. Almost overlapping, isn't it?

CATHY. It wasn't that kind of date.

CRYSTAL. Then it wasn't worth running. (*Indicating glass.*) Go on, drink your medicine before it cools off. (*Cathy takes the shaker and sips. It's much too strong.*)

CATHY. (*A grimace.*) I made it too strong. (*She puts it down. Crystal picks it up.*)

CRYSTAL. Let me taste it. (*She takes a gulp.*) That'll kill the germs all right. Murder 'em. (*Puts the shaker near Cathy.*) Drink it down. Go on. (*Cathy reluctantly takes another sip and puts the shaker down.*)

CATHY. That's enough. I really don't think I have a cold.

CRYSTAL. Now that I think of it, I sneezed on the way over here. (*Takes the shaker.*) Better be careful than sorry, *I* always say. We'll kill the germs together. (*She takes another gulp.*) Your turn.

CATHY. No, I've had enough.

CRYSTAL. I'd appreciate it if you'd drink it, it'll make it easier.

CATHY. Make what easier.

CRYSTAL. (*Heartfelt.*) The reason I'm here in the middle of the night is because I couldn't sleep. My conscience is killing me. If you feel like spitting in my eye, go right ahead.

CATHY. I haven't the faintest idea what you're talking about, Crystal. (*Crystal thinks a moment, then takes the shaker and gulps again. She puts the shaker down.*) I'm waiting, Crystal.

CRYSTAL. When you ran out of the theatre last night you missed the fit Harry threw backstage. He was screaming. I figured the best thing for Crystal was to avoid him. I saw him coming so I ducked into David's dressing room. Who do you think I found in there?

CATHY. Who?

CRYSTAL. The little girl with the school books.

CATHY. What was she doing?

CRYSTAL. Her homework. She's David's sister.

CATHY. His sister?

CRYSTAL. We had a long talk. She's failing in her math and David helps her with her homework during the second act. (*Cathy looks at her a long moment and then picks up the shaker and takes a long drink. Crystal nods approvingly.)* That's right, dear. *(Cathy puts the shaker down. She looks ahead, thinking.)* You can spit in either eye, Cathy. *(Cathy leans back.)* I think people who do what I've done—stink! I know, it's been done to me. Nothing lower! *(A plea for forgiveness.)* But you did ask me, Cathy.

CATHY. *(Deep in thought.)* It's all right, Crystal.

CRYSTAL. *(Unhappily.)* No, it's not all right at all. You two had a real thing going. You make a nice pair, you look like you belong together. You were good casting. And the laughs, you said it was "sensational." That doesn't grow on trees, you know. *(They both think a while.)* I made the trouble, I can unmake it! You got a Bible?

CATHY. *(Still off.)* Uh huh.

CRYSTAL. Let me have it. I'm going to David and swear on the Bible that I made all the trouble with his kid sister. *(She nods.)* I'll play a hell of a scene. I did something like that in stock once. I just have to change a few words around. And it'll work. You know why, because it'll be sincere. I owe it to you. *(Cathy hasn't been listening, lost in her own recalling.)*

CATHY. *(Dreamily, smiling, off.)* David was worried that a man's keeping me.

CRYSTAL. *(Alert.)* Who's keeping you?

CATHY. *(Off.)* He's afraid his wife'll shoot me.

CRYSTAL. Who's shooting you? Who's keeping you? Answer me! Is a man keeping you?

CATHY. *(Now to Crystal, but still in the mood.)* David thinks so. That's what I told him. The man's back in town.

CRYSTAL. *(All clear to her.)* That's how you got him out of here!

CATHY. *(Back to her dreamy smile.)* He's jealous. He was up all night, and he caught a cold, and he was arrested. Very sweet, when you think about it. *(There is the sound of a loud snore from the bedroom. Crystal is startled.)*

CRYSTAL. Who's in there?

CATHY. *(Still in her mood.)* David. He didn't sleep last night. *(Another snore.)*

CRYSTAL. Does he always snore like that?

CATHY. Two short ones and then a long one. Listen. *(A very loud snore from David.)* Now he's turning over on his stomach. He'll sleep like a baby now. *(Sentimentally.)* I'm used to David. I like

40

him. I don't want to break in a new one. Altogether, he's really very satisfactory. (*She considers.*) It's all very satisfactory. I'm going to leave it like this. I'll get my work done in peace and quiet. It's a most suitable arrangement.

CRYSTAL. (*A long look at Cathy.*) You've got it licked, kid. What an idea! A ready made man remover! That's what you've invented! You could patent it and collect royalties! I'm going to do it to Harry! I can't wait! (*Ahead, seeing a vision.*) Every woman's dream! A man in bed, where he belongs. Not in my closet! Not in my bathroom! And picking up his own cleaning! When I want him I tell him the coast's clear and he sneaks over! When I'm through with him he has to leave! That minute! Trained, by God! It's fool proof! (*She picks up the shaker.*) There was another Catherine. Catherine the Great of Russia. Had a whole regiment of soldiers. Took one at a time, from left to right. Never skipped. The first woman libber. Kid, she didn't come up to your navel! (*She raises the glass as a toast.*) To you, girlie—Cathy the Great! (*She drinks. Cathy smiles, pleased, smug.*)

CATHY. Just call me "Your Majesty." (*Crystal puts the shaker down, near Cathy. Cathy picks it up, raises it to toast.*) To equal rights! God bless us! And I'm sure She will! (*She drinks.*)

CURTAIN

41

ACT TWO

SCENE 1

Two days later. Midnight. Cathy is at her typewriter, typing away. She is dressed in rather sheer pajamas. She is a writer who speaks her words aloud as she types.

CATHY. (*Typing.*) You've sold your hair, Marylou? Your beautiful hair! Why? Why? (*She stops typing and looks at her wrist watch.*) Yeah, why? (*Lists the possibilities.*) Food, rent, medicine? Needs money for blood transfusion. Okay. Whose? Mamma? She's on crutches now. Too much. Uncle Harvey? He's in an alcoholic ward. Complicated. The dog! Can a dog have a blood transfusion? Why not? (*Remembers.*) Damn, he was run over last week! (*Considers.*) Who said he was dead? He's been in an oxygen tent. Very pathetic. Next week he goes in an iron lung— (*The downstairs buzzer sounds. She gets up, puzzled, and crosses to the speaker, pushing the activating button. Into speaker.*) Who is it?
DAVID'S VOICE. I'm from the telephone company! May I come up, please?
CATHY. (*Some annoyance.*) What's gotten into you, David? Hurry up here! (*She releases the button. She frowns at this unexpected clowning. She shrugs. Adjusts her hair. Goes to the door, opens it, and waits, to one side, now smiling. Through the door comes David, attired in a coverall of the telephone company's. He carries a tool case. He is wearing a small, familiar moustache. Cathy looks at him in surprise as she closes the door. He faces her.*) Don't tell me, let me guess. You're auditioning for the part of Hitler? Charlie Chaplin? Take that ridiculous thing off!
DAVID. (*Pulling it off.*) Ouch. I glued it on too tight.
CATHY. (*Surveying him.*) What are you made up for?
DAVID. A telephone company repair man. This is my cousin's outfit. (*Indicating the tool box.*) It's real. I thought of it during the performance.
CATHY. I knew you were thinking of something, your mind certainly wasn't on the play. Where did you run after the curtain?

DAVID. Home. To my cousin's place. (*He puts the tool box aside, and will peel off the coverall, which he lets crumple on the tool box.*) I've given our situation a lot of thought. (*Pointing to it.*) If I'd walked through that door just now and your friend happened—just happened—to be here, how would you explain that? (*She just looks at him.*) You couldn't! But a telephone repair man is above suspicion!

CATHY. At midnight? That's above suspicion?

DAVID. I've got an explanation for that. I've thought this all out. This is an emergency.

CATHY. What kind of emergency would bring a telephone repair man here at midnight?

DAVID. (*Triumphantly.*) "We have reason to believe, Miss Temple, your telephone may be bugged! If not you, someone on this trunk line, and I'm sorry but we're obliged by law to investigate this immediately." You know how people feel about bugging nowadays, your friend'd believe that.

CATHY. I told you he's out of town today.

DAVID. He could come back suddenly. You read about things like that in the paper all the time. Husbands, lovers—bang, bang. Where out of town? Philadelphia? That's not far away. By train, it's only—

CATHY. Further than Philadelphia! Are you afraid he's going to find you here and shoot you?

DAVID. (*Stung.*) I haven't got anything to be afraid of. It's you. You're the one who better not be caught.

CATHY. I'm willing to take the risk.

DAVID. Why'd you bring up "shooting"? Does he go hunting? I mean does he know anything about guns?

CATHY. He knows a lot about guns! He was in the war in Vietnam!

DAVID. Listen, I don't care if he walks in this minute! I'd enjoy it!

CATHY. What would you do?

DAVID. I'd say, "How do you do, I'm happy to make your acquaintance." Never hurts to be polite.

CATHY. What would you say twenty minutes from now?

DAVID. Twenty minutes?

CATHY. When he catches us in bed.

DAVID. (*Likes his joke.*) Excuse my back. Ha!

CATHY. Sit down and have a drink, coward. (*He will sit while she makes him a drink at the bar.*)

DAVID. I'm not a coward. I always thought I was, but I'm not.

CATHY. How do you know?

DAVID. I was in Vietnam.

CATHY. (*Surprised.*) Were you? I didn't know that.

DAVID. There're a lot of things you don't know about me. I've done a lot of things.

CATHY. Name one.

DAVID. Yeah, well— (*Thinks.*) I've made a hole in one in golf.

CATHY. My father made two holes in one the same day.

DAVID. I don't believe that.

CATHY. God's truth. July fourth, 1970. He had his picture on the cover of *Golf Digest*. It's framed in his study, with a light over it. He works it into every conversation he can. What did you do in Vietnam?

DAVID. I did what everybody did, I kept my head down. Bullets were flying all over the place.

CATHY. What did you do exactly? (*Forgetting herself, she rattles it off.*) I mean were you in the line, non-com, field grade, company— (*She catches herself.*) I know those terms from a book I reviewed.

DAVID. For a second I thought you were our sergeant. You had the same cadence in your voice. (*He dismisses the coincidence.*) I was a plain GI. A dogface.

CATHY. What outfit were you with?

DAVID. Sixth Infantry, First Battalion.

CATHY. Too bad. It would have been a coincidence if you and my—friend—knew each other.

DAVID. No chance. At his age he was an officer. Reserve type, left over from World War Two. Or One. Spanish American War probably. We didn't see any officers in the mud.

CATHY. (*Slight beat.*) It may interest you to know that more officers, in proportion to their total numbers, were killed than enlisted men.

DAVID. I didn't know that.

CATHY. You know it now. How did you find out you were brave?

DAVID. I never said I was brave, I said I wasn't a coward. That's not the same.

CATHY. The difference escapes me.

DAVID. (*A serious remembering.*) I did what was expected of me. I forced myself. Some fellows did more than was expected of them. *They* were brave.

CATHY. I'll accept that. (*Hands him the drink.*) Will you accept this? (*She kisses him on the top of the head and sits.*) Now drink up and jump in the hay.

DAVID. You've certainly changed the last two days. Do you know that?

CATHY. Really? In what way?

DAVID. I don't know exactly. You're more aggressive. You talk dirty.

CATHY. I always spoke dirty.

DAVID. (*Thinking.*) No, you answered dirty. *I* talked dirty. The man should always start it.

CATHY. We have the vote now.

DAVID. A hell of a lot you're doing with it. (*Now noticing.*) Where's your drink?

CATHY. I'm tapering off. Go right ahead. You're better after a drink.

DAVID. That's what I mean. (*He sips. He thinks. She watches him. Finally.*) What city is he in now?

CATHY. (*Hands primly in lap.*) Washington.

DAVID. But you wouldn't bet your life on it?

CATHY. No. Never bet your life.

DAVID. How do you know he won't walk in now?

CATHY. He always calls me before he comes over. (*Covering all bases.*) When he comes at night. He often comes in the morning without notice though. For breakfast. That's why you can't stay.

DAVID. Damned inconsiderate.

CATHY. His apartment.

DAVID. You said you got it from a girl you knew at Actors Lab.

CATHY. A lie.

DAVID. And you couldn't afford it.

CATHY. Another lie.

DAVID. You're a liar.

CATHY. (*Mildly.*) How dare you.

DAVID. I don't understand women.

CATHY. You bet you don't! Haven't you finished that drink yet?

DAVID. I'm not going to be rushed!

CATHY. You're not fooling me. You like to be begged. You told me once.

DAVID. I did not!

CATHY. Yes, you did. (*Reflects.*) I think it was you.

DAVID. It *was* me! You're driving me crazy!

CATHY. Good! That's the idea. (*A nod of her head toward the bedroom.*) Now? I'll show you crazy.

DAVID. What does he do for a living?

CATHY. Who?

DAVID. Santa Claus!

CATHY. He makes toys.

DAVID. One more answer like that—

CATHY. No, you guessed it, David, by accident. He's a toy manufacturer.

DAVID. (*Surprised.*) He does make toys?

CATHY. (*Loves the challenge of improvising.*) Dolls, electric trains, airplane models. He's very big in military items. Soldiers, tanks, atomic bombs.

DAVID. Atomic bombs!

CATHY. Not real ones. Plastic atoms. Drink up! (*She smiles at him lovingly.*)

DAVID. I'm against military toys. They breed jingoism. (*She puts her arms around him, intimately, kissing him in the ear.*)

CATHY. (*Low.*) As long as you brought up the subject of breeding— (*Ear kissing affects him. He squirms.*) I love it when you play hard to get. (*Still holding the almost finished glass, he enfolds her strongly.*)

DAVID. (*Gutteral.*) Oh, I'm not so hard to get. If you play your cards right. (*Big kissing.*)

CATHY. Sweetheart?

DAVID. Yes, dear?

CATHY. (*Same loving tone.*) You've spilled your drink down my back. (*He pulls back quickly.*)

DAVID. Oh, I'm sorry!

CATHY. (*Getting up.*) Doesn't matter, you can dry me off. Start where you like. (*She starts briskly toward the bedroom, undressing. He puts the glass down and follows her slowly. Over her shoulder.*) First one in bed's boss! (*He shakes his head as he closes the bedroom door. The lights dim to denote a passage of time. They rise again. The door opens and Cathy exits, wearing a robe.*

Behind her comes David, dressed except for his tie, which hangs out of his trousers pocket.)

DAVID. It's never happened to me before.

CATHY. Don't worry about it.

DAVID. Damned embarrassing.

CATHY. You're run down, that's all. You've just gotten over a cold.

DAVID. Could be. I've missed a lot of sleep too. *(He sits. She sits beside him.)*

CATHY. It's quite common. *(He looks at her sharply.)* I understand. You don't eat balanced meals. Take vitamin pills.

DAVID. *(Stung.)* Oysters, whites of eggs and amber powder are the usual recommendations!

CATHY. Your male vanity's showing. I take vitamin pills.

DAVID. Well, stop taking them! Let's even things up!

CATHY. *(Smiles, an idea has occurred to her.)* You've hit on something. There's often an imbalance between the sexual drives of a man and woman. She wants, he doesn't. He wants, she doesn't. I would imagine, offhand, that's made more trouble in the world than all the wars put together. There's a simple solution. Handicap them.

DAVID. Handicap them?

CATHY. Certainly, like horse races. One horse is faster than another and they put more weight on it. In a perfect race all the horses are supposed to finish together. Like in bed.

DAVID. The sex act isn't a contest!

CATHY. Pretty much.

DAVID. Is this what being a feminist means? Turning the most intimate, spiritual moment between a man and woman into an athletic event?

CATHY. Spiritual? You're getting religion into this? Listen, you— man—you! Remember our first rehearsal on this couch? You explained your operation very clearly! "Blitz," you called it! Three meals and flowers! I have perfect recall! Your exact words were "That's par for the course." We got in bed in cold blood! Where did the spiritual come in?

DAVID. *(Wounded, retreats.)* Well, that was a different kind of affair. There are two kinds, Cathy.

CATHY. Let's hear the second kind!

DAVID. The first's sort of, well— *(He searches.)*

CATHY. For laughs. That's what Crystal calls it. Now the second kind?

DAVID. The laughs can grow into something more meaningful. (*Solemnly.*) Like us. (*Cathy looks at him a long moment, and then suddenly her hand darts to her robe pocket and she takes out a handkerchief and puts it to her eyes.*)

CATHY. (*Into the handkerchief.*) You're doing it to me again.

DAVID. (*Dense.*) Doing what?

CATHY. (*Recovering.*) Oh, nothing! Forget it!

DAVID. I'd like to know what brought that on.

CATHY. I said "Forget it!"

DAVID. Women's reactions are a mystery. Always have been. Crazy. Leonardo Da Vinci thought it was the full moon.

CATHY. That's it.

DAVID. What was the other occasion when you cried?

CATHY. (*Runs it together.*) We were in bed and you were asleep and you were snoring and I turned you over on your stomach and you stopped.

DAVID. And that made you cry?

CATHY. You looked so—vulnerable.

DAVID. The moon's full again.

CATHY. It's something atavistic. Millions of years taking care of men, we're conditioned to respond to certain cues. Like Pavlov's dogs. But it'll be bred out of us, don't worry about that. Just give us a few more generations.

DAVID. But meanwhile?

CATHY. What do you mean, "meanwhile"?

DAVID. What about Santa Claus?

CATHY. What about him?

DAVID. I don't like him.

CATHY. You don't know him.

DAVID. I don't have to know him to not like him. It's atavistic. Why can't you give him up? We can move in a place without wall panelling. (*She looks at him endearingly. She puts her hand on his arm.*)

CATHY. (*Earnestly.*) David dear. Let's leave it the way it is. It's comfortable.

DAVID. It isn't for me.

CATHY. Because you can't have breakfast in the morning?

DAVID. (*A burst.*) No, goddamn it! (*Pointing to the bedroom.*)

Why do you think I couldn't perform in there? I'm not run down, and it's not my cold! I could have double pneumonia! A hundred and ten fever wouldn't stop me!

CATHY. You'd be dead at a hundred and ten. A hundred and eight.

DAVID. You're an insensitive numbskull!

CATHY. (*She looks at him a moment.*) You're bothered by Santa Claus?

DAVID. Certainly I'm bothered by Santa Claus! If you like a girl you don't want to share her!

CATHY. But a man can play the field?

DAVID. For laughs! For laughs! Not when he's stuck on someone! (*Cathy looks at him for a long, searching moment, since this is what the play is about. Finally, she pats him on the thigh.*)

CATHY. That's a good mark for you, David. A very good mark.

DAVID. (*A tone of resignation.*) Okay, I'll marry you. (*Cathy is watching him carefully. He has his elbows on his knees, staring ahead dejectedly.*)

CATHY. The condemned man ate a hearty meal.

DAVID. Well, you get the message.

CATHY. I get the message. No, thank you, David, but I appreciate being asked. Every girl likes to be asked. (*She pats him again.*) That's another good mark for you.

DAVID. Listen, stop giving me brownie points! You're not marking my report card! What's wrong with being married? We were living that way before!

CATHY. (*Earnestly.*) David dear, it's not the right time for us to be tied down now. We're both trying to make it in the world. Can't we go on like before? Let's try it for a year. (*David stares at her.*)

DAVID. How much of a sex hold has this man on you?

CATHY. It's not that.

DAVID. Well, what the hell is it? Are you just afraid of hurting his feelings?

CATHY. (*Grasping at the tack.*) That's it. He's sweet and gentle. It'd break his heart. If you met him you'd like him.

DAVID. The hell I would!

CATHY. You would.

DAVID. I'd punch him on the nose.

CATHY. I wouldn't do that. I once saw him—I wouldn't do that.

49

DAVID. When did he start with you? Pretty early. You said he supported you through college.

CATHY. Did I say that?

DAVID. Yes, you did! I have perfect recall! Do you know he's guilty of statutory rape?

CATHY. Oh no!

DAVID. Oh yes! You were under age! An anonymous letter to the district attorney'd fix everything, and I'm thinking about it!

CATHY. We weren't lovers. We're companions.

DAVID. (*Indignant.*) You're not going to insult my intelligence and say he's paying your rent for conversation? You're not that witty!

CATHY. Well, we're *mostly* companions. If you'd stop talking about him it wouldn't bother you so much!

DAVID. That's it. That's a woman. Sweep everything under a rug.

CATHY. (*Housewife now.*) When did I ever sweep anything under a rug? You've seen me clean this place often enough! The only time *you* cleaned, when I had a sick headache, *you* swept everything under the rug.

DAVID. (*Hands up.*) It was just a figure of speech. God, you women are touchy nowadays.

CATHY. We were always touchy! We didn't have enough guts to answer back before!

DAVID. It was better before. I was born too late. Eighteen hundred was a good year.

CATHY. It would have taken more than three meals and some flowers to get me in bed then! You can't have it both ways! (*He thinks for a long time.*)

DAVID. I have a suggestion.

CATHY. Let's hear it.

DAVID. I accept your assessment of the toy manufacturer. The picture is clear to me. A sweet, gentle man with an invalid wife. Calls you daughter, helps you through college, father image, you feel obligated. I can understand that.

CATHY. Thank you.

DAVID. He must be a reasonable man, that successful. Fair, tolerant.

CATHY. (*Pleased the way it's going.*) He is that.

DAVID. I'll talk to him. That's the solution.

CATHY. That's not the solution.

50

DAVID. I'll explain what we mean to each other. He'll bow out gracefully. Probably give us his blessing.

CATHY. Forget it.

DAVID. Why not? What's wrong with it?

CATHY. I couldn't introduce you. It would spoil everything.

DAVID. (*Thinks a moment.*) All right, I have another suggestion.

CATHY. Let's hear it.

DAVID. You don't introduce us.

CATHY. So far, good.

DAVID. I meet him accidentally.

CATHY. For what purpose?

DAVID. I'd like to appraise him. It wouldn't take me too long to know his character. I took a psychology course.

CATHY. I thought you were an architect.

DAVID. They include a psychology course.

CATHY. What for?

DAVID. So you know how much to charge clients. Let me size him up, I'll know how to handle him.

CATHY. (*Shakes her head.*) You're on the wrong tack.

DAVID. The simple truth is you don't want to break off your relationship with him!

CATHY. That's right. (*The doorbell buzzes.*)

DAVID. Who's that?

CATHY. (*Flat.*) It's him. Hide in the closet.

DAVID. I hope it's him! (*A thought.*) I'll hide under the bed! That'd surprise him! At the right time! (*Cathy goes to the door.*) Give him a heart attack! (*Cathy opens the door and Crystal enters.*)

CRYSTAL. I heard you on the stairs. I'm not interrupting anything?

DAVID. Yes, you are!

CATHY. David, that's rude.

CRYSTAL. I'm interrupting a damned dull argument. I tried to listen through the door but I couldn't hear much.

CATHY. It's teakwood, not a nail in it.

CRYSTAL. (*Oblivious.*) Can I sleep here toninght? Harry and I had a fight.

CATHY. Of course you can.

CRYSTAL. Thank you. Go on, keep arguing, I can hear now. (*The phone rings and Cathy goes to it.*)

DAVID. *You* may not be sleeping here tonight!

CATHY. (*Into phone.*) Hello? Hello, Harry. (*She looks to Crystal.*)

CRYSTAL. (*Loud.*) I'm not here!

CATHY. (*Into phone. Listening. To Crystal.*) He says he heard you.

CRYSTAL. Is he calling me a liar? (*She goes to the phone, takes it from Cathy. Forcefully.*) Drop dead! (*She bangs up.*) No one can say I'm not reasonable. Well, where did we leave off? (*The phone rings again as she takes a step away. She returns to the phone and picks it up.*) Drop d—e—a—d—dead! (*She has heard something. To Cathy.*) It's for you. Washington.

CATHY. (*Hurrying to the phone.*) Oh dear!

DAVID. Now's the time for "Drop dead!"

CATHY. (*Into phone.*) Hello . . . That was my girl friend . . . She thought you were her boy friend . . . Oh, marvelous! What time tomorrow? . . . No, I'll make you lunch here . . . But I'd like to . . . Yes, I'm sure. How does lamb stew strike you? . . . Plenty of boiled onions . . . Light on the carrots . . . Can't wait to see you. 'Bye. (*She bangs up. The phone rings immediately. She picks it up.*) Hello? . . . Well, I don't know, Harry . . . (*Crystal goes to the phone cord and pulls the portable plug from the wall.*)

CRYSTAL. He'd keep it up all night. You should see my phone bill. (*David rises.*)

DAVID. Very well! You've made your choice! I withdraw my offer!

CATHY. We're only going to have lunch.

DAVID. Eat hearty! Light on the carrots! Good bye!

CATHY. Good bye, David. (*He picks up his tool box and coveralls and strides to the door, opens it, and goes through it dramatically. He just closes it when we hear quite a noise from outside.*) What's that?

CRYSTAL. (*Going to the door.*) He fell over my suitcase. (*Cathy stands where she is, defiant, arms folded. Crystal opens the door and looks. Calmly.*) He's out cold. He hit his head on the stair railing.

CATHY. (*Running to him.*) Oh God!

CRYSTAL. (*Reporting.*) He's moving. (*Cathy disappears, Crystal holds the door, and soon David appears, holding his head, helped by Cathy. She steers him to the couch.*) I'm sorry.

52

DAVID. (*Being led.*) Leaving a suitcase in front of a door! Of all the stupid things to do—

CRYSTAL. (*Getting her overnight bag.*) I didn't know whether I could stay. I didn't want to seem pushy. (*She puts the bag near the bedroom door.*)

CATHY. (*Feeling his head.*) You've got a fine bump!

DAVID. (*As she touches it.*) Ouch! Don't touch it!

CATHY. (*Going to the kitchen.*) I'll put some ice on it.

DAVID. (*Shouting.*) I don't want any ice on it!

CATHY. (*From the kitchen.*) Without ice you'll have a bump tomorrow they'll see from the last row!

CRYSTAL. Good character touch. Doesn't fit the plot though. Of course they could write a line to cover it.

DAVID. Oh, shut up!

CRYSTAL. Charming. (*Cathy exits with a dish towel in which she has put ice cubes.*)

CATHY. Get your hand away. (*He does. She presses the iced towel on it.*)

DAVID. Ouch!

CATHY. Sit still.

DAVID. (*Ungraciously.*) I can do it! (*He holds the towel to his head. The girls survey him.*)

CRYSTAL. You're lucky you have a hard head. Harry had to have three stitches.

CATHY. He fell against a stair railing?

CRYSTAL. Ketchup bottle.

DAVID. (*Getting up.*) I'm perfectly all right. (*He rocks on his feet though.*)

CATHY. Sit down, you're still shaky. (*David throws the towel down, male like on the couch, and Cathy picks it up.*)

DAVID. I don't know why it should concern you. (*He starts toward the door. They watch him. He turns from the door.*) You'll never lay eyes on me again!

CRYSTAL. What about in the play?

DAVID. (*Making the best of it.*) That doesn't count.

CATHY. Take a taxi.

DAVID. (*Loftily.*) I have a car!

CRYSTAL. If it's the car out front the police were towing it away.

DAVID. Oh no! (*He runs through the door. We hear a crashing noise, this time featuring a metallic sound.*)

53

CATHY. (*To Crystal, who is in line with the open door.*) What happened?

CRYSTAL. (*Reporting what she sees.*) He fell over his tool box. (*Cathy would go, but Crystal continues.*) He's all right, he's getting up. (*We hear him bounding down the stairs. Crystal goes to the door and closes it, talking.*) They were only jacking the car up. Maybe he can stop them. (*Cathy crosses to the window and looks down.*)

CATHY. Too late. There it goes. (*Watches further.*) Now David's chasing it. He'll never catch it. (*Further report.*) He's dropped the tool box. The tools spilled out. He's picking them up. (*Turns back.*) He's all right, he was running pretty fast.

CRYSTAL. Did I come at the wrong time?

CATHY. No, right time. We weren't seeing eye to eye.

CRYSTAL. I sneezed on the way over. Do you mind if I ward it off a little?

CATHY. It's your scotch. Be your guest. (*Crystal will fix herself a large drink at the bar.*)

CRYSTAL. What's he mad about?

CATHY. (*A tiny, pleased smile.*) He's not happy about the man who's keeping me. Not at all.

CRYSTAL. Would you like to hear Harry's reaction?

CATHY. You told Harry someone was keeping you?

CRYSTAL. Uh huh. I did it great, too. Rehearsed it in the bathroom for half an hour. Told him this man'd been keeping me for years.

CATHY. What did he say?

CRYSTAL. His exact words?

CATHY. Uh huh.

CRYSTAL. "He owes two months rent."

CATHY. No!

CRYSTAL. I was out of ketchup bottles. Lucky for him. We were in bed, actually. I tried for the lamp but I couldn't make it.

CATHY. You were in bed when you told him?

CRYSTAL. That's the best place, usually, if you're going to spring something on a man. You didn't come off so good either?

CATHY. Oh, it'll be all right.

CRYSTAL. David was pretty mad on the way out.

CATHY. I'll work on him. During the play. We've got some sexy scenes together. He— (*She smiles.*) can be managed.

54

CRYSTAL. Atta girl. Hit 'em below the belt. (*A moment, while Crystal gulps scotch.*)

CATHY. I want to ask you something, Crystal.

CRYSTAL. I'm right here.

CATHY. Would you marry a man who—

CRYSTAL. (*Interrupting.*) Yes.

CATHY. I haven't finished the sentence.

CRYSTAL. He wouldn't either.

CATHY. Pay attention, Crystal.

CRYSTAL. Right on.

CATHY. David— (*Reluctant to phrase it baldly.*) can't—well, perform.

CRYSTAL. Oh, he isn't a very good actor, but he's still learning. He'll be all right.

CATHY. In bed!

CRYSTAL. (*Now alert.*) David? I don't get it. I thought you said it was sensational?

CATHY. You're not following me.

CRYSTAL. Well, you're underplaying everything! Out with it!

CATHY. I believe—in these circumstances—a man who—can't— is to be admired.

CRYSTAL. I don't know what the hell you're driving at but it's nothing to be admired! They can have many faults, and they all do, but the one they mustn't have is that one! I stand on that!

CATHY. He can't because of the other man!

CRYSTAL. (*A light.*) Oh! Oh, I see. (*She shakes her head.*) That's very sensitive. (*Nods.*) Yes, it is.

CATHY. (*Fondly recalling.*) He doesn't want to share me. He said we could move in another place without panelling. He's even willing to marry me. Reluctant, but willing. When you think about it— (*Crystal has been trying to halt the lip quivering, fails, and her face contorts into a grimace of crying.*)

CRYSTAL. It didn't bother Harry! (*She goes quickly in her purse for her handkerchief.*)

CATHY. Now, Crystal—

CRYSTAL. There's the difference between them. That's the most touching thing I've ever heard of in my whole life!

CATHY. (*While Crystal blows.*) Yes, it is touching, isn't it? He does have character. I don't know what to do about it. I mean I feel responsible for his condition.

CRYSTAL. He'll work it out himself.

CATHY. (*Attentive.*) How will he work it out?

CRYSTAL. He's only got this ailment because he loves you. He'll be all right with anyone else.

CATHY. You can't tell. I've read about these things. Men get blocks. It would be terrible if it was permanent.

CRYSTAL. (*A shrewd glance.*) If it'll relieve your conscience—only because you're a friend—I'll remove the block. (*Cathy eyes her, expressionless.*)

CATHY. You lay one finger on him and I'll kill you with my bare hands.

CRYSTAL. Just testing. You've got it bad, girl.

CATHY. He's mine and I'm going to keep him.

CRYSTAL. Well, what's your problem? Marry him.

CATHY. I'm not ready for marriage.

CRYSTAL. What have you got to get ready?

CATHY. I want another year of being on my own. You're married all your life.

CRYSTAL. Not necessarily.

CATHY. I'm going to be.

CRYSTAL. (*An admiring look.*) You probably will. You're the type. God, I wish somebody'd marry me. Anybody!

CATHY. You put on a big act, Crystal. You wouldn't marry anybody you didn't love. And you don't sleep with all those people you say. You tell lies.

CRYSTAL. I didn't come here to be insulted. I was insulted pretty good today though.

CATHY. This is going to be another lie.

CRYSTAL. No, this one is on the level, for a change. Depressed me all day. My agent asked me to lunch. He's got a thing for me but I avoid him. See, you're right, I'm not a bad girl. He beat around the bush for a while and then he says, "How about a porno movie?" That's a ploy they use to get started. They figure after a porno movie anything they suggest is like a handshake. I don't like pornographic movies. I said, "No, thanks, I don't care to see one." He said, "I didn't mean see one, I meant be in one."

CATHY. (*Horrified.*) Oh, Crystal! What did you do?

CRYSTAL. You know me, never at a loss for words. I said, "Excuse me, I have to go to the ladies' room" and I walked out of the Russian Tea Room. Left a goddam good lunch. Borsht and blinis. I was crying on the bus, everybody was watching.

CATHY. I'm sorry, Crystal.

CRYSTAL. (*An effort to brighten.*) So that's why I'm selling marriage today. (*Cathy has a far off look on her face.*)

CATHY. I'm just kidding myself. I couldn't stand it, Crystal. I just couldn't.

CRYSTAL. Marriage isn't terrible. Lots of people are married.

CATHY. I couldn't stand someone else curing him of his—ailment. I won't stand for it.

CRYSTAL. (*Carefully.*) What are you going to do about it?

CATHY. I'm curing him myself. I'm taking him off the market. Permanently.

CRYSTAL. You're marrying him?

CATHY. I have to, Crystal. I can't take the chance of losing him. I love him. (*Crystal gets up, goes to Cathy and kisses her gently on the cheek.*)

CRYSTAL. (*Choking it down.*) I'm not going to cry. (*They look at each other fondly.*) Cathy, you're the first woman in the history of the world who's marrying a man because he couldn't. And it's not going to catch on. (*The scene blacks out.*)

ACT TWO

Scene 2

One P.M. the following day. Colonel Temple, in his shirt sleeves, is eating at the table, across from Cathy. She wears a fetching yellow dress. His coat is over the back of his chair. There is a casserole on the table and a bowl of fruit.

Temple eats for a while. He watches Cathy, whose mind is elsewhere. Cathy idly spears a bit of lamb, brings it almost to her mouth, and returns it to her plate.

TEMPLE. Is that some sort of new diet?

CATHY. (*Brought back.*) Excuse me, Dad?

TEMPLE. You keep bringing the fork to your mouth but you don't go any further.

CATHY. I'm sorry, I—I guess I'm distracted.

TEMPLE. Perfectly all right. I respect the creative process. You're thinking of your radio program?

CATHY. Uh, yes.

TEMPLE. Mother follows it religiously. Unfortunately I'm in the field when it's on.

CATHY. You wouldn't like it. You need dishpan hands to listen to it.

TEMPLE. Mother fills me in with the plot. What's Marylou going to do about the fatherless baby?

CATHY. She's not going to have it.

TEMPLE. An abortion?

CATHY. Abortion's not allowed on daytime radio. It's a network rule. Only after six P.M.

TEMPLE. Well, how does she not have it?

CATHY. It turns out it was a false pregnancy.

TEMPLE. In the eighth month?

CATHY. Actually, it's the eleventh month.

TEMPLE. An eleven month pregnancy?

CATHY. The people who listen to our program don't count very well. It's dramatic license. Like comic strips. Little Orphan Annie's been ten years old for thirty. It's accepted.

TEMPLE. I see— (*He resumes eating. Cathy is distracted again.*)

CATHY. (*Finally.*) Dad—

TEMPLE. Yes, dear.

CATHY. If, by some chance, I got married in New York, would mother come to the wedding?

TEMPLE. On her surf board! Are you telling me something?

CATHY. No, no, I was just speculating. I—I've had a tentative offer.

TEMPLE. (*Interested.*) Have you? The baseball cap? (*She nods.*) What's suddenly made him desirable?

CATHY. Oh, something. Something. I'm only turning it over in my mind. It's unlucky to hatch chickens before they're counted. Or the other way around. I'm not very clear this morning.

TEMPLE. No, you're not. You were reading the paper upside down.

CATHY. Was I? (*Smiles.*) I brushed my teeth with cold cream.

TEMPLE. Ho ho. He's got you winging.

CATHY. Well, he's winging too.

TEMPLE. (*He leans forward.*) You can trust ol'Dad, sugar.

CATHY. It's nothing definite. You'll be the first to know. After David. That's his name.

TEMPLE. (*Puzzled.*) You haven't told him he's marrying you?

CATHY. Not yet. He's asked me, but not strong enough.

TEMPLE. I see. I think I see.

CATHY. I want a stronger ask.

TEMPLE. A stronger ask. Well, that's fair. It's not clear, but it's fair.

CATHY. Just trust me. I'm in the negotiating stage.

TEMPLE. Do I tell mother anything? She'll ask questions.

CATHY. Not just yet. Hide it for awhile. I'll keep in touch.

TEMPLE. Hiding things from your mother isn't easy. Do you know she asks me questions when I'm asleep? In a soft voice. I answer without waking up.

CATHY. (*She likes that.*) Really? I'll have to remember that.

TEMPLE. I don't know what she's found out. I hope it's nothing military. If the Russians ever capture her we're in trouble.

CATHY. They'd be the ones in trouble.

TEMPLE. Yes, they would.

CATHY. (*Looking at her watch.*) I'm afraid it's time for me to go to the radio station.

TEMPLE. You haven't eaten anything! You have to have something in your stomach.

CATHY. I have butterflies.

TEMPLE. They're not enough. Take a few mouthfuls.

CATHY. I couldn't swallow.

TEMPLE. You're in love all right.

CATHY. Could you eat when you courted mother?

TEMPLE. I couldn't afford it.

CATHY. I feel awful leaving you when I see you so little. That lamb stew isn't worth a two hour visit.

TEMPLE. (*He loves her.*) It is though.

CATHY. Would you like to ride in the cab with me to the radio station?

TEMPLE. A staff car is picking me up here in half an hour. Don't worry about me, I'll do the crossword puzzle. (*Crosses to kiss him.*)

CATHY. Tell mother I love her.

TEMPLE. I'll do that.

CATHY. And remember I love you.

59

TEMPLE. I'll remember. (*She picks up her purse and starts to the door.*)

CATHY. When I know you'll know. The door locks when you close it. (*They wave at each other and she's out. He helps himself to more stew. He takes the newspaper, folds it, reaches for a pen from his coat on the chair. He pours another cup of coffee. He puts sugar in it, looking at the puzzle. He stirs. He fills in a word. He sips. He begins to eat, still puzzling, and the doorbell buzzes. He puts his fork down, goes to the door, and opens it. There stands David, in the coveralls and the moustache, carrying the tool kit.*)

TEMPLE. Yes?

DAVID. (*Looking at the card in his hand.*) Telephone company. You Catherine Temple?

TEMPLE. No, she's shorter. She just left.

DAVID. I've got an appointment to check her phone.

TEMPLE. Well, she's not here. Would you mind coming back later?

DAVID. This was the appointment. I don't know when I can come back. Not this week.

TEMPLE. (*Considers.*) Very well, come in. (*David does.*) I'm having my lunch.

DAVID. I won't disturb you.

TEMPLE. You only missed her by a minute.

DAVID. I may have seen her leaving the building. Girl in a yellow dress, in a hurry?

TEMPLE. That's right.

DAVID. (*Looking at his card.*) You say you have this strange buzzing and you hear a lot of clicking?

TEMPLE. I don't say anything. I've spoken on the phone, I didn't hear any buzzing or clicking.

DAVID. Well, that's what she reported. The phone may be bugged.

TEMPLE. Bugged? Her phone?

DAVID. If not hers, somebody else's on her trunk line.

TEMPLE. Are they still doing that?

DAVID. Never stopped. It's worse than ever.

TEMPLE. You'd think they'd have learned their lesson, wouldn't you? (*David has been scrutinizing his rival. Temple looks squarely at him.*) Haven't I seen you some place?

DAVID. I don't think so.

TEMPLE. You haven't been in the army recently?

DAVID. Not recently.

TEMPLE. You look vaguely familiar.

DAVID. People often tell me that. (*Temple goes back to his lunch, David goes to the typewriter desk with his tool box. He lifts the telephone and looks at the bottom professionally. Temple is eating.*)

TEMPLE. You said you weren't in the army "recently." How recently?

DAVID. Vietnam.

TEMPLE. What outfit?

DAVID. Sixth Infantry, First Battalion.

TEMPLE. Chu Lai. You did your share.

DAVID. (*Flat.*) Yes sir.

TEMPLE. Have you had your lunch?

DAVID. No, I haven't.

TEMPLE. Join me. There's more than enough. It'll only go to waste. (*He pushes Cathy's plate aside, dumps the rolls and puts that plate in place. Also the fruit fork.*)

DAVID. (*Surprised.*) I couldn't do that. It's against company policy.

TEMPLE. Why is it? You're entitled to a lunch hour. I insist. Mark it up to good customer relations. I also happen to be an A.T. and T. stockholder. Ten shares. Not the majority stockholder but technically I'm your employer. Come on now. (*David joins him warily. He does not want to like this man. Temple takes his plate and gives him a generous helping.*) Dig right in!

DAVID. (*Reluctantly.*) Thank you.

TEMPLE. (*Eating.*) Little better than K rations and mess kits, hey?

DAVID. Little better. (*He watches David take his first bite.*)

TEMPLE. Pretty good, huh? My daughter made this. She's a great cook.

DAVID. (*Can't eat. Puts the fork down. A sneer, flat.*) Your daughter.

TEMPLE. She's an actress. She's appearing in a play right now, got a smash up review in The New York *Times*. That's a show business term— (*Notices.*) Why aren't you eating?

DAVID. I'm not really hungry.

TEMPLE. Don't you like lamb stew?

DAVID. (*Getting up and returning to the phone.*) I'm allergic to it.

TEMPLE. Is that so? I'm sorry. I didn't know people had lamb allergies.

DAVID. They do.

TEMPLE. Can I get you something else? Make you a ham sandwich?

DAVID. (*Short. This isn't turning out right at all.*) No, thank you. (*David screws off the rim of the phone earpiece and looks at it in what he thinks is a professional manner. Temple is curious, and saunters over, hands in his back pockets. David takes the pen clipped to his breast pocket and taps the receiver. He holds it to his ear and keeps tapping it.*)

TEMPLE. Find anything?

DAVID. Can't tell yet.

TEMPLE. (*Happy to have found someone he can talk soldier to.*) How long were you at Chu Lai?

DAVID. (*Busies himself with the phone inspection.*) Four months.

TEMPLE. What were you?

DAVID. (*Occupied always with the phone.*) Rifleman. C for Charlie platoon.

TEMPLE. Were you at Hill 76?

DAVID. Yes, I was. (*David screws back the rim on the earpiece.*)

TEMPLE. That was something. I've read some conflicting reports about that battle. Tell me about it.

DAVID. I was in a trench. All I know is what I read in *Newsweek*. (*He now starts to dial the phone. Into phone.*) Hello. I'd like to speak to Supervisor Cousins. (*Temple idly picks up the long telephone cord.*) Hello, Mister Cousins? . . . This is George Spelvin. I'm at the Temple apartment checking out that bugging possibility. (*Temple has idly gathered up the cord to keep it from tangling and now comes to its free end. He looks at it, puzzled, while David, his back to Temple, goes blithely on. Obviously David can't be talking to anyone.*) My opinion is that it's situated in the trunk line. That is, if it *is* bugging . . . It could be a cable malfunction, but I haven't a magnetizer to verify that . . . I'd need a double deck magnetizer number three. Maybe number four . . . (*Temple eyes David's back, and looks him over, for size. He looks around for a weapon, to be safe, although man to man he'd do fairly well. His eye settles on the putter against the wall. Calmly he goes to it, will pick it up, and return to David.*) What do you suggest? . . . (*David's back is to Temple, he is unaware of the approaching putter.*) I've opened the grid . . . Both grids . . . There may be relays in the basement but I can't test them without authorization . . . Service would be cut off for an hour and the subscribers would have to be notified— (*Temple, quite at ease, but alert, holds the grip to David's back, in simulation of a gun barrel.*)

TEMPLE. (*Even, low.*) Stand perfectly still. Don't move one muscle! (*David is rigid for a moment and then slumps. Temple expertly feels David's pockets, still behind him, for any weapons. Satisfied that he is unarmed, he changes to holding the putter at the grip end.*)

DAVID. (*Down.*) You don't have to shoot me.

TEMPLE. Turn around slowly. (*David does. Holding the putter easily, but at the ready.*) I'm very good with a putter. I'm a scratch golfer.

DAVID. It's my putter. (*David reaches to his lip and pulls off his moustache.*) There! (*Temple is still in the dark.*) Don't you recognize me?

TEMPLE. No, I don't.

DAVID. I'm the actor who plays opposite Cathy! (*Temple peers at him. He lowers the putter.*) That's why you thought I looked familiar.

TEMPLE. There's some sort of explanation due me, boy. What are you doing here?

DAVID. (*Disgusted with himself.*) I don't know what the hell I'm doing here! I've been hanging around, and I saw Cathy leave, and I wanted to take a good look at you. I didn't think further than that. I haven't been thinking clearly lately.

TEMPLE. (*Considers, makes up his mind.*) You're lucky you were with the Sixth Infantry. Sit down while I (*He turns to go back to the table.*) finish my lunch. (*David trails after Temple, dejected.*) Eat something.

DAVID. No, thank you. (*Temple resumes eating. David sits.*)

TEMPLE. Begin at the beginning. Why did you want to take a look at me?

DAVID. You know, you're not the kind of a man I expected.

TEMPLE. What kind of man did you expect me to be?

DAVID. (*Shakes his head.*) Lecherous, I guess. (*Temple stops his fork mid-air.*)

TEMPLE. Lecherous!

63

DAVID. That's not the word.

TEMPLE. It better not be!

DAVID. (*Making up his mind.*) I'm going to take a big risk!

TEMPLE. (*Colonel tone.*) You've already taken a big risk today. I'd be careful of the next sentence. Why did you want to take a good look at me, and answer me directly.

DAVID. I love Cathy.

TEMPLE. (*Looks at him sharply a moment.*) So do I.

DAVID. I hope you do. It would be unforgiveable if you didn't. (*This doesn't make sense to Temple.*) I love her more than you do.

TEMPLE. (*Annoyed.*) That's debatable.

DAVID. You knew her first. You know her longer. I admit that.

TEMPLE. What do you mean you admit it? Of course I know her longer! (*Another long look.*) How did you get out of the army? On a Section Eight?

DAVID. What's that?

TEMPLE. A medical discharge!

DAVID. No, I finished my hitch.

TEMPLE. (*Patiently, but steely.*) I'm going to continue eating my lunch. I'm not going to say one word. If you haven't explained yourself by the time I've finished you're going to regret it!

DAVID. I know all about you and Cath. She didn't volunteer it, I got it out of her. (*A breath.*) She told me that you're keeping her. (*Temple looks up sharply.*) I accept that. It bothers me, I'm not happy about it. You don't like to hear that another man is paying the rent, and charge accounts, for the girl you love but the way I look at it, it happened before we met, and what's passed is passed, and I say let bygones be bygones. (*Temple opens his mouth to say something. David holds his hand up.*) You said you weren't going to say anything. I'd like to go on. (*Temple closes his mouth. He does not continue eating.*) She loves you. Not the way she loves me, I've every reason to believe. She feels gratitude to you mostly. You're a rich toy manufacturer, you sent her through college, that was very generous. And I can even see the situation through your eyes. Your invalid wife, hurt on a surfboard—

TEMPLE. (*Startled.*) When was she hurt on a surfboard?

DAVID. Cathy didn't say. I assume it was years ago. Don't you remember when?

TEMPLE. (*Recovering.*) I thought you meant recently.

DAVID. She's not still riding on a surfboard?

TEMPLE. She tries.

DAVID. That's very courageous of her.

TEMPLE. Yes, it is.

DAVID. I would like to appeal to your better nature.

TEMPLE. Shoot.

DAVID. You've been good to her, in your way. You've been re-paid. Amply. Search your heart, do the right thing, release her and let her marry me.

TEMPLE. You've asked her?

DAVID. I have.

TEMPLE. And what did she answer?

DAVID. She doesn't want to hurt your feelings. She says you're sweet and gentle and it'll break your heart. (*A look at Temple.*) You don't seem sweet and gentle to me.

TEMPLE. Well, I am.

DAVID. You want her to be happy, don't you?

TEMPLE. Why would she be happier with you?

DAVID. I'm going to marry her!

TEMPLE. Marriage is no guarantee of happiness. Every couple in a divorce court once thought it was and they were wrong.

DAVID. (*Sincerely.*) I'll take care of her all my life.

TEMPLE. Now we're getting to the nitty gritty. I feel some responsibility for Catherine. What, young man, exactly are your prospects for taking care of my— (*Almost a slip.*) young friend?

DAVID. (*Marshalling them, but slightly uncertain.*) Yes, well, my prospects. First, I love her—

TEMPLE. We've covered that. Besides love.

DAVID. I have an acting job—

TEMPLE. You're a terrible actor!

DAVID. The New York *Times* doesn't think so!

TEMPLE. They're wrong! I saw you! You couldn't remember your lines!

DAVID. That was the second night.

TEMPLE. Are you only supposed to remember your lines every other night?

DAVID. That was an accident, it never happened again. I'm also an architect!

TEMPLE. You are? Then what are you doing making faces at people?

DAVID. The art of acting is more than making faces at people.

TEMPLE. I'm sure it is, but the art of acting is also a very precarious way of making a living. (*David looks at him and leans back, thoughtfully.*)

DAVID. There's a lot in what you say. I'll tell you a little secret. I've discovered I'm not a very good actor.

TEMPLE. It's not a secret.

DAVID. "Clean and incisive" isn't bad, that's what the *Times* called me, but it's really not enough to raise a family on. I've decided that recently.

TEMPLE. You've made a wise decision.

DAVID. I'm a very *good* architect. I was the head of my graduating class. I've got half a dozen offers from top firms.

TEMPLE. (*Interested.*) Have you?

DAVID. But I'm not going to take any of them.

TEMPLE. Why not?

DAVID. I've got a commission to re-do an off-Broadway Theatre. That's an untapped field. Most of the theatres in this country are obsolete. I'm going to specialize. Having been an actor I know what's needed. Convertible stages with movable aprons, new acoustical materials, adjustable sight lines, remote control light boards, horizontal scene docks—

TEMPLE. I take your word for it.

DAVID. (*Lost in his vision.*) I'll be the only actor-architect in the profession! I'll have a monopoly! I couldn't take all the jobs!

TEMPLE. Don't overwork yourself. Go on.

DAVID. I've talked this over with Cathy. She's encouraged me. (*He recalls.*) I've got a feeling she doesn't think I should keep acting.

TEMPLE. *She* ought to be the critic on the *Times*.

DAVID. Anyway, I can support Cathy. (*Temple lets himself smile.*)

TEMPLE. Let's say you can.

DAVID. Then I have your approval to marry Cath?

TEMPLE. You'll have trouble with her father. He's a tough old bird.

DAVID. You know him?

TEMPLE. Intimately. Do you know what he does for a living?

DAVID. What?

TEMPLE. He's a Colonel in the regular army. Hard man.

DAVID. I didn't know that.

TEMPLE. (*Nods.*) Yep. When he finds out you two have been carrying on he may horsewhip you. (*A thought.*) Where do you get a horsewhip nowadays?

DAVID. Why doesn't he horsewhip you?

TEMPLE. Good question.

DAVID. He'll never know about Cathy and me.

TEMPLE. I won't tell him if you don't.

DAVID. I'll get around him. I'm a good salesman.

TEMPLE. Yes, you are. You come from a big family?

DAVID. Four brothers, one sister.

TEMPLE. Four boys? Is that so?

DAVID. One of my brothers is a line backer for the Jets.

TEMPLE. (*A reflex.*) He is? Is *he* married?

DAVID. (*Nods.*) Uh huh. Has two kids. Why do you ask?

TEMPLE. Forget it. Football talent isn't hereditary. Do you play golf?

DAVID. I once made a hole in one.

TEMPLE. Did you? Really? (*He smiles at the opening.*) Commendable. Would you believe I made *two* holes in one the same day? (*David stares at him. The realization will sink in as Temple continues.*) I did. It was on July fourth, 1970. My picture was on the cover of *Golf Digest.* I've got it framed in my study.

DAVID. With a light over it.

TEMPLE. (*Chuckles.*) That's right. Wouldn't you put a light on it? (*David stands up and runs his hand through his hair. He is reviewing the past deceptions.*) *Golf Digest* said the odds of making two holes in one in the same round are a million, four hundred thousand sixty seven to one. They figured it out on a computer.

DAVID. (*He smiles, grimly.*) That much?

TEMPLE. It's mostly luck, you know. Any hole in one is luck. A lot of professionals have never made any. Two the same day, well, you see the odds.

DAVID. How's the toy business lately? (*This non-sequitur throws Temple a moment.*)

TEMPLE. It's all right.

DAVID. You carry any puppets? Puppets on a string?

TEMPLE. (*Puzzled but obliged to go along.*) We've got a good line of puppets.

DAVID. You have any about five feet ten?

TEMPLE. (*Stalling.*) I don't think they come that big.

DAVID. Oh, they do. I know one, I've seen one. I was wondering if it was yours?

TEMPLE. No, we don't handle that size.

DAVID. It was nice to have made your acquaintance, Mister—I'm afraid I don't know your name.

TEMPLE. It's—Smith. (*David fits his two names in at the same time as Temple says "Smith."*)

DAVID. Smith or Brown. (*David smiles.*) I knew it had to be one. A married man doesn't give his right name.

TEMPLE. (*Amused.*) No, he doesn't.

DAVID. I'm happy to have had this talk with you.

TEMPLE. So am I.

DAVID. You've been very helpful, and I appreciate it. Not everyone in your position would have been so—understanding.

TEMPLE. I was young once myself. If you're curious, you've made a very good impression on me.

DAVID. Thank you.

TEMPLE. I've decided to put in a good word for you with Cathy's father.

DAVID. That's very generous of you. Well, I'll be going. (*He gets his tool box.*)

TEMPLE. It's possible we'll see each other some time again. You never can tell.

DAVID. No, you can't. It's a small world.

TEMPLE. Isn't it?

DAVID. (*At the door.*) Good bye, Mister Brown.

TEMPLE. Smith.

DAVID. (*Smile and wave.*) Well—

TEMPLE. Good bye. (*David is out. Temple beams. He goes to the phone, plugs it in, and dials his home in Hawaii directly.*) Martha? . . . I'm in New York. I'm in Cathy's place. She's not here. Listen closely. (*He hums the first few bars of Mendelsohn's "Wedding March."*) Hello, grandma. Time to get off the surf board . . . No, no, she's not married. It's coming up though. Any minute . . . Easy, girl, easy . . . Yes, I've met him . . . Well, he's not good enough for her, of course . . . Nice looking boy . . . Has a brother who's a line backer for the Jets . . . I said—never mind. Nice looking boy! Not too bright, an ideal son-in-law . . . Architect, full of beans, he'll take care of her. He loves her, I can tell you that. He's put up with more than I would . . . Now, now, I didn't mean it that way, Martha. Well, that's the bulletin, I'll be home tomorrow . . . What? . . . How would I know a thing like that? . . . (*A meaningful smile.*) Did your parents know about us? . . . They did? . . . How did they know? . . . You told them! . . . You mean to tell me you actually told them— (*She's hung up. He hangs up.*) I always wondered how I got accepted that quickly. (*The scene blacks out.*)

ACT TWO

SCENE 3

The same night. Midnight. Dark stage. The door opens, Cathy and David enter, Cathy switching on the lights. Disposes of purse, fixes her hair.

CATHY. Fix you a drink?

DAVID. No thanks.

CATHY. Do you feel like eggs? Make you an omelette, I've got those little frankfurters you like.

DAVID. No, I ate a big meal before the show. I'll watch you eat though.

CATHY. I'm not hungry. Since when do you eat before a performance?

DAVID. My appetite's suddenly come back. I was off my feed for a couple of days.

CATHY. Maybe that's made the difference in your acting. You were very good tonight.

DAVID. Would you say I was cleaner or more incisive?

CATHY. I thought you attacked the role differently. You were more, well, assured. Sort of cocky, in fact.

DAVID. It's boring to play the part the same way all the time.

CATHY. You chuckled a lot.

DAVID. I was characterizing.

CATHY. In strange places. Where chuckles didn't belong.

DAVID. Matter of interpretation. I thought *you* were rather subdued, as long as we're being critical. (*She sits. He will.*)

CATHY. I know I was.

DAVID. You feeling all right?

CATHY. (*Heavily.*) I'm all right. Physically.

DAVID. Where aren't you all right?

CATHY. Mentally. I'm torn. That's the word.

DAVID. Torn?

CATHY. Torn. Which is why I asked you up here. And it was very nice of you to come, considering. I need a friend's advice.

DAVID. I'm a friend.

CATHY. I know you are. That's one of your best qualities. Friendship.

DAVID. Thank you.

CATHY. I haven't forgotten your concern for me the night of the Rainbow Room.

DAVID. Forget it. What's bothering you, and how can I help you?

CATHY. I received a special delivery letter this morning. From him.

DAVID. Him? Who? Oh, your landlord.

CATHY. He's not my landlord.

DAVID. I was being delicate. Your lover, if you insist.

CATHY. May I read it to you?

DAVID. Isn't it personal?

CATHY. Yes, but I want you to have the whole picture. Your advice is very important to me.

DAVID. Okay. (*She gets up to go to her writing desk, will open a drawer and take out a letter. David, as soon as her back is to him, smiles and shakes his head at this new ploy.*)

CATHY. (*During the return cross.*) I'll read it to you without inflections. I don't want to influence you.

DAVID. That's the best way. (*Cathy holds the letter before him, but not too long.*)

CATHY. Look at his handwriting. Not very steady.

DAVID. (*Looking.*) Looks all right to me.

CATHY. It's wavery. He usually writes more boldly.

DAVID. Well, you'd know.

CATHY. (*Showing him a corner.*) What are these stains? Do you think they're tears?

DAVID. (*Looking.*) Could be soup.

CATHY. Soup!

DAVID. He might have written it during lunch.

CATHY. This letter wasn't written during lunch! Wait 'till you hear it!

70

DAVID. I'm listening.

CATHY. Dear Kitty Cath. That's what he calls me.

DAVID. Kitty Cath? Cute.

CATHY. (*Strong.*) I take my pen in hand with strong emotion.

DAVID. You're inflecting. (*Cathy looks at him sharply. She doesn't care about these interruptions.*) You were going to read it straight, so I wouldn't be influenced.

CATHY. Frankly, it's not his emotion I'm reflecting but my own.

DAVID. Excuse me. Continue.

CATHY. (*Resuming.*) This is the most difficult letter I've ever written. It is not written lightly. It is written in heart's blood. Why has our relationship dwindled to cool companionship? Where have I failed you? Have you found another? I sense you have. Over the years I have tortured myself with the prospect that this might happen one day. Do not tell me if it has. I could not bear to hear it. (*To David.*) How can you tell me to keep my emotions out of it?

DAVID. Do the best you can.

CATHY. (*Continuing.*) Has this intruder discovered your virtues; your tender heart, your cheerful disposition, your common sense, your homemaker ways? (*A simulated deprecating smile to David.*) He exaggerates a little.

DAVID. (*Gallantly.*) Not at all.

CATHY. Well, thank you. (*Continuing.*) What has he offered you? Marriage, I am sure. The one gift I could not bring you. (*She looks at David.*) Here comes the sad part.

DAVID. It's been pretty sad up to now.

CATHY. (*Resuming.*) I have spoken this over with Charlotte, my wife—

DAVID. Doesn't he know you know his wife's name?

CATHY. (*A slip.*) I'm only reading what's written. Don't forget he's upset.

DAVID. (*Nods.*) Keep reading.

CATHY. —and we've come to a decision. Since we have been man and wife in name only for all these years our life together has been merely a convenience. She is willing to divorce me. She would like to travel. Of could I will provide for her handsomely. She will have the teddy bear factory—

DAVID. (*He didn't expect this.*) Teddy bear factory!

CATHY. He's the largest teddy bear manfacturer in the country.

DAVID. Go on.

CATHY. —and this, plus a trust fund, will keep her in comfort and, indeed, luxury. I, therefore, hereby, feel free to ask your hand in marriage. Will you marry me? And whatever your decision is I will always be grateful for the gay companionship—which is what our relationship mostly has been—you have generously bestowed upon me. I can say no more. I await your answer. Hopefully. (*She puts the letter down and looks at David expectantly. He looks at her, expressionless.*) Now you know why I gave a poor performance tonight.

DAVID. It was a pretty good performance.

CATHY. What do I tell him? (*He looks at her a long time. She waits. He gets up.*)

DAVID. Do you mind if I have that drink now? (*As he turns to the bar Cathy glares at him. This is not the reaction she expected.*) Fix you something?

CATHY. (*Short.*) No, thank you.

DAVID. (*Fixing the drink.*) You wouldn't think there was that much money in teddy bears, would you?

CATHY. This letter is not about teddy bears!

DAVID. Certainly he mentions teddy bears. He's giving Charlotte —his wife—the teddy bear factory. Read it again.

CATHY. This letter is about a man asking to marry me!

DAVID. I'll get some ice. (*He enters the kitchen. Cathy gets up, her hands on her hips. It's going all wrong. David speaks from the kitchen.*) Your refrigerator needs defrosting! (*We hear the refrigerator door closing. David returns, the ice cubes in the glass.*) The light's out in the refrigerator too, homemaker.

CATHY. I didn't ask you up here to discuss my electrical appliances. Didn't this letter affect you?

DAVID. You're damned right it did! I'm letting some time go by so I can get some perspective and advise you intelligently.

CATHY. (*Relieved.*) Oh, I see.

DAVID. We're talking about your life. Your future. Let's not be hasty.

CATHY. You're right.

DAVID. (*Sitting again.*) The man who wrote that letter isn't a toy manufacturer.

CATHY. He isn't?

DAVID. No. He's a poet!

CATHY. Well, it's written from the heart.

DAVID. (*Sipping.*) The poor bastard.

CATHY. (*Sitting.*) I feel terrible.

DAVID. You should feel terrible. You've an obligation to him.

CATHY. Yes, I have.

DAVID. (*Solomon in judgment.*) Of course you have an obligation to yourself.

CATHY. (*This is better.*) That's true.

DAVID. You don't marry a man just because it suits him.

CATHY. No.

DAVID. You have to think of yourself. Gratitude isn't a basis for marriage.

CATHY. (*Things are going fine.*) No, it isn't.

DAVID. He's older than you. A good deal older. What of the future?

CATHY. I've thought of that.

DAVID. Ten years from now, twenty years. You can't beat Mother Nature you know. Think of that.

CATHY. I've been thinking of it.

DAVID. You'll be playing chess. In separate bedrooms.

CATHY. That would be difficult. (*A long pause. Cathy waits.*)

DAVID. Still—those twenty years. Very juicy. You'd be sitting pretty.

CATHY. (*Alarmed.*) What do you mean?

DAVID. Be realistic, Cath. Rich man, adores you. A lot of trimmings come with that Christmas tree. Don't believe that bird in a gilded cage propaganda. That's a song. Life's not a song. Life's hard, life's real. (*Cathy is horrified. David takes a long sip.*) You want my advice? Marry him!

CATHY. That's your advice?

DAVID. What's bothering you? The chess playing? (*Meaningly.*) There are other games, on the side.

CATHY. I don't follow you. I hope I don't. Are you saying you'd expect me to cheat on him?

DAVID. (*Evidently he does.*) Well—

CATHY. I happen to believe in fidelity in marriage! Forever!

DAVID. I do, too. I'm glad you said that. Marriage is—sacred. Which is why I'm surprised your admirable friend is ditching his wife.

CATHY. (*Caught.*) It's a marriage in name only.

DAVID. Because she was hurt on a surf board. What happened to "For richer or poorer, in sickness or health"? There's nothing in either Testament that exempts surf board accidents. No, she's getting the dirty end of the stick.

CATHY. (*Doing the best she can.*) She wants to travel.

DAVID. She *says* she wants to travel. She's sacrificing herself. Fine woman. *She'll* be on your conscience. (*Cathy is stumped, David is thinking of her problem, she believes.*) Of course, there's another option.

CATHY. (*Hopefully.*) There is?

DAVID. (*He nods.*) What's wrong with keeping this same arrangement? Go on like before. (*Indicating.*) He pays for the—panelling, and those little charge accounts. Everybody's happy, nobody's hurt. (*Cathy is very depressed, looking ahead unhappily. David watches her, unobserved, with great satisfaction.*) Something's bothering you. I know what it is.

CATHY. (*Down.*) You do?

DAVID. You're thinking about me. Aren't you? How I feel about it? (*She looks at him.*) Don't worry about it. I've got it licked.

CATHY. You've got what licked?

DAVID. My non-performing. I'm over it. It's all in your mind, you know.

CATHY. (*Ice.*) What happened to your not wanting to share me with another man?

DAVID. I had a long talk with myself. I discovered I was very unreasonable. You're a modern woman. Free, liberated, a man's equal. But was I an equal man? No, I wasn't matching you. My reaction was a throwback to the old fashioned morality. I wanted you for myself. I was possessive. A real male chauvinist. I admit it. You know something? The problem you women have is not with yourselves, it's with us. We men'll have to do the adjusting. I had no right to own you exclusively. No sir. And once I saw it in that light, why, my inhibitions disappeared. (*He puts the glass down.*) And Cath, I'm going to prove it to you! (*He advances on her.*)

CATHY. Don't you lay a hand on me!

DAVID. What's the matter?

CATHY. I don't want to!

DAVID. (*Wrestling.*) Just give me a chance.

CATHY. (*Resisting.*) No, David, no!

DAVID. (*Continuing.*) Turn the ignition on, the motor'll start running.

CATHY. (*Fighting him off.*) No, no! I don't want any motor running! I'm not in the mood! (*David stops.*)

74

DAVID. Maybe you're the one who's run down? Oysters, white of eggs and amber powder work for women too.

CATHY. I'm tired, David. Would you please go?

DAVID. Have I said something to offend you?

CATHY. Yes, you have.

DAVID. You're not very consistent. Isn't this the relationship you've been selling me?

CATHY. I've changed my mind.

DAVID. Full moon again.

CATHY. That's right. Good bye.

DAVID. (*Shakes his head. Gets up.*) Maybe Da Vinci understood women. I don't.

CATHY. It was easy for him. He was a homosexual.

DAVID. There are advantages. I'm thinking about it. Well, I'll just run along.

CATHY. Do that.

DAVID. See you at the theatre tomorrow. The show must go on, you know.

CATHY. I'll be there. (*He starts toward the door, and the phone rings. He looks at it. She goes to it.*) Hello? . . . Hello, mother. How are you? (*David smiles wryly.*) No, I can't recognize it, what *are* you humming? Mendelsohn's wedding March? What for? . . . Daddy told you? . . . Told you what?

DAVID. (*Shakes his head.*) Ah, too bad. I was going to draw this out a few days.

CATHY. (*Looking at David.*) He met him . . . He approves of him . . . You always wanted an architect. (*Her hand on the phone. Shining eyes, a statement of love.*) You son of a bitch!

DAVID. (*So is this.*) Flattery'll get you no place.

CATHY. (*Into phone.*) No, we haven't set any date . . . Yes, it'll be in a church.

DAVID. *My* mother'll like that. You'll like my mother. (*She is trying to refrain from crying and isn't succeeding. David strolls to her.*)

CATHY. I'll call you when I know exactly . . . I promise . . . (*David gives her his handkerchief and kisses her on the forehead. She blows, listening to mama. David goes to the couch, sits, and takes his shoes off. Cathy watches him. He slips his tie off.*) The minute I know the date I'll call you . . . (*She pantomimes to David by shaking her head negatively, waving her finger at him. He stops, thinking it's a refusal. Cathy points at the bedroom. She's a girl who likes to be comfortable. He nods. Gets up, starts to take his trousers off.*) Yes, mother . . . Yes, mother.

DAVID. (*One leg out of his trousers.*) First one in bed's boss.

CATHY. (*Seeing her chance. Quickly.*) I have to go now, mother! Something's come up! I'll call you tomorrow! 'Bye! (*She hangs up and runs to the bedroom. David starts after her but can only hobble with the inhibiting trousers.*)

DAVID. You little sneak— (*No use, she's beaten him into the bedroom, and always will.*)

CURTAIN

PROPERTY LIST

ACT ONE—*Scene 1*

On Stage:
Framed sketches of stage sets
Water colors and oils
Desk, with:
  Typewriter and paper
  Pile of new books
  Telephone, with long cord
Table, with light chairs
Easy chair
Sofa bed
Shelf of books
Group photographs (framed)
Bottles of liquor and glasses, on bar

Off Stage:
Scripts (2)

ACT ONE—*Scene 2*

On Stage:
Pair of sneakers (men's)
Baseball glove, on chair
Man's sweater and tie, on back of chair
Baseball cap, on lamp
Golf putter, against L. wall
Golf balls (2) beside putter
Empty champagne bottles, on table
Empty champagne glasses (2)
New York *Times*
Book
Notebook, with pencil clipped to it, on bar
Pajama bottoms (men's) under sofa cushion

Off Stage:
Copies of New York *Times* (5)
Suitcases (2)

77

On Stage:
Breakfast dishes, on table
Suitcase, near door
Tray
Tablecloth
Jigger and bottle of rum, on bar
Martini shaker

Off Stage:
Tea kettle, in kitchen
Bottle of scotch, in paper bag

Act Two—*Scene 1*

Off Stage:
Tool box
Overnight bag
Dish towel and ice, in kitchen

Personal:
Wristwatch (Cathy)
False moustache (David)
Handkerchief (Cathy)
Handkerchief, in purse (Crystal)

Act Two—*Scene 2*

On Stage:
Dinner plates, coffee cups, silverware, on table
Casserole ⎫
Bowl of fruit ⎬ on table
Newspaper

Personal:
Pen (Temple)
Appointment card (David)
Pen (David)

Act Two—*Scene 3*

On Stage:
Letter, in desk drawer

Off Stage:
Ice cubes

Personal:
Handkerchief (David)

NEW
PLAYS

LONELY PLANET
by Steven Dietz

THE AMERICA PLAY
by Suzan-Lori Parks

THE FOURTH WALL
by A.R. Gurney

JULIE JOHNSON
by Wendy Hammond

FOUR DOGS AND A BONE
by John Patrick Shanley

DESDEMONA, A PLAY ABOUT A
HANDKERCHIEF
by Paula Vogel

*Write for information as to
availability*
DRAMATISTS PLAY SERVICE, Inc.
440 Park Avenue South   New York, N.Y. 10016